DUSTY WINDOWS

A Collection of Stories and Accounts of Growing Up on
a Farm in Oklahoma during the Dustbowl and
Depression Years

©Roger Lee Duncan   1996
0103 Glenwood Avenue
Carbondale, Colorado 81623

Publication Design:
Network Graphics, Denver, Colorado

Printed in the United States of America

1st Printing
June 1997

Cover Art: Matt Duncan
Back cover photos: Matt Duncan and Rachel Duncan
Traditional photos collected:
    Mary Haggard and Jennifer Duncan
Editing: Brenda Duncan
Marketing: Nicola Frost

ISBN: 0-944918-03-4

Dusty Windows

A Collection of Stories and Memories of Growing Up on a Farm in Oklahoma during the Dustbowl and Depression Years

Life passes by my dusty windows;

As each scene grows and subsides,

I await that precious moment

When an image stops and abides.

Roger Lee Duncan

DEDICATION

This collection of stories is dedicated to the farmers and townspeople of Butler who stayed put during the Dustbowl days and became my heroes; and, especially, to my own heroic family, then and now.

Roger Lee Duncan

ACKNOWLEDGMENTS

Special thanks go to my wife, Brenda, who has been so supportive and helpful in the development and editing of this collection. Brenda experienced life as a displaced child in wartime England, which seems to have given her an understanding of some of the struggles of growing up during the 1930s and '40s in Oklahoma.

I am grateful to my four children, Jennifer, Matthew, Nicola and Rachel and other members of my family, who have encouraged and helped me recount my joys and tribulations of growing up in a very different place and time from here and now. Our son Matthew provided the drawings and design for the front and back covers of this book.

A special debt of gratitude goes to Andy Cleary, a dear friend and president of Network Graphics, who helped steer us through the mysteries of publishing and saw the publication of this collection of memories through to its final printing.

A final word of thanks goes to Charles Moore who was kind enough to read through the final manuscript with some pithy editing.

                                                                                                        R.L.D.

FOREWORD

I was born on a farm near Butler in western Oklahoma in1922 and was graduated from Butler High School in 1940. My childhood and youth were quite normal for someone growing up on a farm, except for the intrusions of a depression, a dustbowl and a world war. The effects of the people around me and the environment of the times were apparently profound as evidenced by my rather vivid recollection of life among them.

The stories and accounts contained in this collection are representative of the memories I have of my early life. Typical of accounts of influences on my youth is "Memories of the Dustbowl". The following lines were written by Brenda Duncan in response to these memories.

> *Dust on the windows,*
> *Dust on my bed,*
> *Outlined on my pillow*
> *Where I rest my head.*
>
> *Dust on the crops,*
> *Dust in the sky,*
> *Dust on the fences*
> *Three wire high.*
>
> *Dust over everything.*
> *Where is the rain?*
> *Our dust blows off to Kansas,*
> *Then comes back again.*

TABLE OF CONTENTS

PROLOGUE

During the 1930s and 1940s, Butler was a busy, vibrant town of about 400 people. There were four grocery stores doing a bustling trade and a number of other businesses supporting an energetic community. Oklahoma State Highway No. 33 ran East and West through the main part of the town and intersected Main Street.

Going south down Main Street, on the west side of the street were Simpson's Grocery, the drug store, the hardware store, Word's Grocery, and the Butler Herald. On the other side of the street going south were Smith's Grocery Store and Produce, the movie house, the barbershop, the Five & Dime and the Butler Hotel. To the north on the west side of the street were the bank,

McClure's Grocery and Produce and Ben Nye's furniture store; on the opposite side of the street were a produce house and G. Small's blacksmith shop. A second blacksmith shop was located also on the north side of town.

To the east of the intersection were the A.L. West Lumber Company and a full-service filling station. Down the highway to the west sat the 33 Restaurant, the jail, a filling station and two automobile garages. On the outskirts of town were two cotton gins and a grain elevator, along with other enterprises. There were two excellent medical doctors in town and a very stable bank.

Butler was a country town in western Oklahoma. It developed by serving the farm community and its residents, and was dependent upon the farm community for its survival. The term "trading" fit perfectly here. Farmers brought their cream and eggs to the produce places and bought food and other home supplies from grocery stores. Farmers sold cotton to the gins and grain to the elevator. Major repairs could be obtained from the blacksmith shop and from the automobile shops. (The blacksmith would also grind corn or wheat for cooking purposes upon request). Construction materials and other farm supplies could be obtained from the lumberyard.

The farmland around Butler is best termed as marginal. There are some bottom lands of creeks and streams that are fertile, but most of the uplands have very thin soil, and the rainfall renders the climate as semiarid. Our family struggled to survive there in the 1930s and 1940s on a 240-acre farm. The following stories and accounts are built around my memories of Butler and the surrounding community during this period.

MEMORIES OF THE DUSTBOWL

*There was nothing comfortable nor romantic
about the Dustbowl.*

It began in earnest in 1934 when I was 12 years old and lasted in its meanest form for about three years. I understood, even then, the factors that created the Dustbowl, beginning with the long drought that affected the Great Plains. *

Cultivated plants withered and died in the hot, drying winds, leaving much of the finely granulated soil unprotected from erosion. Persistent winds picking up grains of the open soil created the dramatic horror that remained with us all too long.

The most horrific of these dust storms occurred in April of 1935. I remember the lines of black clouds towering to tens of thousands of feet and approaching from the North. Large flocks of birds flew frantically in front of the bank of clouds; many people revealed later they thought the end of the world had come.

The winds accompanying these fronts were a persistent source of discomfort and irritation. They picked up the dust and

---

* The Norman, Oklahoma <u>Transcript</u> reported the annual rainfall for the region to have dropped from 20.90 inches in 1930 to 9.69 inches in 1935. The least amount for this period was 8.62 inches in 1934.

blew it swirling into our clothes and faces, and the dust seemed
to permeate every thing and every activity that was a part of our
lives.

The dust lifted by the cutting winds settled in drifts like
brown snow dropped during a winter blizzard. The taller drifts
built up along barbed wire fences already clogged by rolling, dry
tumbleweeds. The drifts were often as high as the tops of the
fence posts.

When the winds subsided, the dust remained suspended in
the air. It was eerie, and quiet and dark. Automobiles driven at
mid-day kept their headlights on, appearing like a pair of candle
lights in a dirty fog. Houses in those times, particularly farm
houses, were not well insulated against the cold or the dust. I
recall waking many mornings to find a layer of fine dust across
my pillow, outlining where my head had lain. I remember, vividly
and gratingly, the layers of dust on the furniture and on the
linoleum covering the kitchen floor. I have memories of foot-
prints left in the dust on the kitchen floor and, despite Mom's
care in preparing food, the grinding of dust as we ate our meals.

Most of the people living in our area seemed to understand
the wide spread effects of the dustbowl, and that it was not going
away overnight. One of our neighbors would say, too often to be
funny, "Well, there goes Kansas down to Texas. But, don't worry,
it'll come back by tomorrow." The Kansas City Star, a weekly
newspaper delivered in the mail, reported that our dust had traveled through the upper winds as far as the state of Virginia. The
term "Black Blizzards" came to be used to describe the dust
storms.

The dust had a disastrous effect on the growth of all cultivated plants. We tried each year to grow crops, most often to find
they obtained minimal growth or simply dried on the stalk. The
farm expression, "I couldn't even get my seed back" applied most
generally. We knew the fatality of our crops when Dad told us to
turn the cattle and horses into the cultivated fields for pasture.

Our efforts to survive the dustbowl often seemed to be futile
or at best a subsistence action. We cultivated the crops as soon as
we could after a rain, to cut down the evaporation of precious
water in the soil by stopping capillary action. This plowing was
done when the soil was dry enough to crumble and was intended to create a dust mulch. It was thought to be one of the most

important practices in dry land farming. In the open fields we harrowed strips of land to block the removal of soil from the fields by the wind. Later, this type of cultivation was credited with being one of the major causes for the dust particles to be picked up by the wind. The shallow layer of topsoil was pulverized. Modern techniques include deep plowing that leaves vegetation and larger clods in the top layer of soil.

In response to the devastation of these years, the federal government promoted long range conservation programs such as paying farmers to build farm ponds and to terrace their lands to slow the runoff of water. Farmers were paid to let their land lie fallow to provide ground cover and to enrich the soil. The Civilian Conservation Corps (CCC, a program for unemployed youth) built shelterbelts, strips of deep rooted trees to break the flow of the winds. The CCC was obviously a joint product of the Depression and the Dustbowl.

The negative effects of the Dustbowl slowly subsided in the late 30s, more at the whims of nature than the efforts of people and governments, I am sure. It is good to believe, however, that our seeming minor human efforts at ending the Dustbowl were part of the recovery.

Two questions remain for me. The first is whether Humankind has learned enough from the dustbowl to prevent its recurrence. The second one is academic; did the simultaneous happening of the depression and the dustbowl, ironically, help us survive, with the depressed cost of living paralleling the loss of farm productivity? I was not aware of an accompanying loss of human spirit. There was yet a quality of life, which might be questionable by today's standards, but had virtues beyond the experiences of modern society.

The parallels between those early black clouds and the brown ones I now encounter in Denver, Colorado are gripping. Both are the works of Man and nature, with Man being rightfully accountable for their creation.

Note: I remember the call of the Raincrow, "Ooh, ooh; ooh ooh; ooh, OOH, ooh. I could never see this bird, but I always thought its call signified hope, that rain was coming. The voice seemed far away, even though it was actually close by. When the dove took off with a whistling sound, she took with her the hope for a refreshing summer shower.

CANNING FOOD FOR THE WINTER

How do you feed a family of two adults and five growing children during a harsh winter on a farm which has no electricity, no running water, no gas for cooking or heating, no growing plants and little or no income? During the 1930s and 40s, my mom, with a little help, did it quite well.

During the summer and fall months, Mom canned anything edible that could be canned. It was all stored in an earthen cellar on shelves lining its walls. I could review much of the summer by going down in the cellar and counting the quart and half gallon glass fruit jars filled with ready foods.

There were jars of green beans, tomatoes, snapped and shelled black eyed peas, a lot of cream style corn, peaches, pickled cucumbers, pale wild plums, wild grape juice and even wild lambsquarter and polk salat greens. There were jars of canned meats, packed unattractively in a hardened sea of lard, but with the saving thought of its being served hot and brown.

As I recall, canning food wasn't easy, requiring considerable amounts of labor for various steps in the process, and careful attention to details. Often a neighbor lady, usually Byna Wright, worked with Mom to do the canning. Fortunately, the food to be canned matured at differing times, allowing for specific processes for differing foods, and much needed respites from the arduous tasks of canning. Knowing there would be food for us during the winter also helped us through canning days. We five children, with Dad's occasional help and supervision, gathered the food to be canned and brought it to the house.

We picked bushel baskets of green beans, tomatoes and cucumbers from a garden spot along the creek, the best piece of soil on our farm. We picked baskets of black eyed peas growing between rows of cotton. We gathered gunny sacks of corn from the field across the road.

Wild purple grapes draped from vines growing on the trees lining the creek, and we searched along the creek banks for poke salat plants, whose roots look like asparagus roots and are cut beneath ground level. We also had a thicket of wild sand plums on a slope about a quarter of a mile west of our house and currants along the creek banks. We picked lambsquarter greens in the early spring wherever we could find them, which was just about anywhere.

Preparing the food for canning also involved the children. We all snapped green beans, usually in the dining room. I remember the handfuls of whole green beans lying on a dishtowel across my lap. I learned to snap the ends off the beans and pull the end down the edge of the bean to remove the "strings" one pod at time, snap those that were tender and shell those that were too mature for snapping. I dropped the results back into my lap among the whole pods. I always was pleased to finish a lapful and to dump my finished mound of snaps and shelled beans into the large gathering pot. We usually sat in a circle, often involved in conversation and enjoying the community gossip between Byna and Mom.

We shucked and silked the corn outside the kitchen door, and then Mom or Byna would cut the kernels from the cobs. I was always amazed at how dexterous they were. The first cut down the ear of corn was almost exactly half way into the kernels, and the second one went down to the cob. After these double cuts around the ear of corn were completed, they scraped the cobs with knives and dumped the kernels and scrapings into the collecting pot. Invariably, there was a considerable amount of silks in the final product, which we all accepted. In those days, corn was not bred specifically for human convenience and consumption.

The actual canning of food was done in the kitchen by Mom, sometimes assisted by Byna. My role in this process often was to prepare the kerosene cook stove for the operation and to draw a supply of water from the cistern. The stove had four burners arranged in one row and was fed through a pipe from the kerosene tank at the right end. Each burner had a cylindrical wick which could be adjusted in height to control the amount of heat. Each wick needed to be trimmed to give a constant efficient flame. On the top of each burner sat a cylindrical metal chimney with an Eisenglass window to show the height of the flame.

The stove wasn't vented, and the south kitchen window was usually lifted a crack for fresh air. Fortunately the house wasn't insulated, and we survived the potential hazards of the kitchen stove.

On canning days the stove operated in full force. Glass jars were sterilized in pans of boiling water along with their lids and rubber rings. Food to be canned bubbled on one of the burners. And for certain foods, a pressure cooker whistled away. I was amazed what Mom knew about canning, including which food needed to be placed in the pressure cooker for preservation, and what could be "cold packed". What I knew about canning was limited to the fact that the jars were always sterilized. I was impressed that Mom, who weighed about 90 pounds, could tighten the jar lids so well they were almost impossible to remove when we tried to open the jars a few months later in preparing a family meal.

On canning days the fumes from the stove were overpowered by the smells of canning, especially on pickling days when the pungent smells of fresh dill and of vinegar permeated the neighborhood, or on those days Mom canned plums or grape juice.

On cold, snowy winter evenings, it was comforting to have Mom ask one of us to go to the cellar to bring up a jar of corn, or pickles, or plums for a cobbler. Mom and Dad may have worried about our well-being during the Depression and Dustbowl days. I never gave it a second thought.

Precious Water

Providing water for family living during the Dustbowl years presented a real and persistent problem. Water from our shallow well down by the creek had so many minerals in it as to make it unusable for washing clothes or for cooking. It was used to water the animals. Many of the minerals came from the gypsum deposits in the oil.

Soap combined with our well water formed an ugly scum that greeted us any time we attempted to wash something. I once tried to wash my hair using well water and Proctor & Gamble's P&G soap. I was horrified at the gooey mat it produced on my head. Mom rescued me with a vinegar rinse that was, at best, half-effective in removing this horrible mess. Detergents were not on the market then, but I doubt their effectiveness in shampoos combined with the gyppy waters from our well.

The water that sustained personal and family life came directly from the rain or snow. We collected it from the roof of our house and stored it in two hand dug, concrete lined cisterns, one for the south side and one for the north side of the house.

Each cistern had a concrete box above ground level about three feet square with a wooden top and a hinged door. When we needed water for the house, we took the metal water bucket form the kitchen out to one of the cisterns, snapped its bail onto the cistern rope, lowered it into the water, giving it a snappy pull to one side to sink it and, by hand, pulled the bucket of water up out of the cistern.

The cistern water was cool and nice and prized. To keep the water good, we would stir it regularly by raising a full bucket of water a few feet above the level of the water in the cistern, and dropping it repeatedly back into the water. To clean the cisterns periodically, we would use all the water from one of them, climb down into it on a ladder and scrub it out. It was a full family operation, with some pulling up the refuse, bringing clean water from the other cistern, some scrubbing and rinsing the cistern floor.

I was always amazed at what we found on the bottom of the cistern, which measured about 12 feet across. There was invariably a water bucket that had come loose from its rope, or was still snapped to the rope. There was a layer of mud usually about two inches deep, containing an occasional pencil or comb that had fallen out of someone's shirt pocket as he or she bent over to sink the water bucket, and, sometimes, the carcasses of small animals that like to live in cool wet places.

I hardly wonder at the expression that the only thing less sanitary than a cistern is a cesspool. But I don't recall any ailments we had that were related to cistern water. I remember the joy of a cool drink from the fresh bucket of water in the kitchen, removed from the unknown depths of the cistern. If the bucket was near empty, it was tempting to set the dipper down carefully and quietly, lest Mom would hear and tell the last user to go out and draw a bucket of water. She often ended her request with "If the house burned down, the first thing to burn would be the durned water bucket."

NEW HOME SCHOOL

New Home School was located 6 miles north of the town of Butler. We lived a mile and a half south of the school, which was housed in a white wooden building consisting of two rooms. Grades one through four were in the 'little room' and five through eight in the 'big room'. There was a movable partition between the two rooms and a stage at the far end of the 'little room'. The school house became a theater for Christmas programs, for church on Sundays and for prayer meetings on Wednesday nights.

Each room had a large heating stove which would burn wood or coal. One of the teachers' responsibilities was to fire up the stoves in the morning during the wintertime and to keep them going during the school day. The church deacons took care of heating for church meetings.

There were four outbuildings: two privies, a barn for the horses that children rode to school and a small cottage to house the teachers. The cottage was located on the school grounds across from the privies and the barn.

Typical of most rural schools of the 30s, the walls of the school displayed pictures of George Washington (Stuart's unfinished painting) and of Abraham Lincoln. There were other paintings including "Man with Hoe", "The Gleaners" and a picture of trees reflected in a pool. There were no displays of student art. The flags of the United States and of Oklahoma were presented on staffs at the front of each room.

Desks and their seats were screwed onto two parallel boards that spanned the length of the classroom. There were four or five rows of these seats, and the teachers could move them for easy cleaning of the floors. There was a groove at the top of each desk to hold pen or pencil, and a hole to the right for an ink well. There was a shelf under the top of the desk to store books, writing stuff and other personal belongings.

The library for the 'big room' was housed in one metal cabinet about six feet high and three feet wide. I remember the clanging noise the door made when I closed it and turned the metal latch, even though I closed it slowly to keep from disrupting the work of other students and to avoid the teacher's disapproval. One of the main treasures of the library was The Book of Knowledge, a 20 volume set of encyclopedias.

The teacher scheduled short periods for reading, history and arithmetic for each grade level, and if I was not involved directly, I could either listen to the assignment, do homework or go to the library. I read all of the 20 volumes of the Books of Knowledge during grades five through eight, acquiring a considerable knowledge of history, geography, and science. I even learned how to make a paper cube through origami paper folding. When the teacher said, "Will the fifth grade class come forward for arithmetic", I knew it was time to raise my hand and ask for permission to go to the library.

I have often thought about the blessings and faults of attending a two room rural school for the full eight year commitment. It is moot now, as it was then. I have no complaints. Despite the dearth of materials and specialists, I suspect Jean Piaget, noted Swiss psychologist, would heartily approve of the opportunity I had to become an 'agent of my own learning'. However, if I had a choice of sending my own children through the New Home school system or a contemporary one with well equipped classrooms, I could have an interesting conversation with myself.

SCHOOL LUNCHES

When I was growing up on the farm, I never thought of school lunches as needing to be nutritious or attractive. They were something to help one get through the day, or as my mom would say, to "keep body and soul together until you get back home".

In our family, each child put together his or her school lunch as hurriedly and expeditiously as possible after the morning chores were done, and before the one and a half mile walk, or horseback ride, to school. Biscuits and salt cured bacon or ham from the breakfast table often helped fill the lunch menu along with apples or peaches from the orchard or tomatoes and carrots from the garden.

If we had to go to the pantry to find stuff for lunch, there was always the staple, dark Karo syrup or jelly and peanut butter for a sandwich. You might find gingersnaps or homemade cookies there. "Sandwich Spread"; a combination of mayonnaise, pickles and other vegetables spread, on homemade bread often had to suffice as the main lunch item. Our school lunches would hardly start you drooling at 11:30 in the morning. One of the positive attributes of our fare may have been that mornings seemed short-er without great expectations for lunch.

A part of the joys of noontime, however, was the trading of lunch items with other students. It provided a real challenge for me to trade up and to diversify my meal. There were two kinds of kids who were prime targets for trades, the relatively rich and the very poor.

One relatively affluent family brought what I believed at the time to be great lunches to school. Most of us felt their mom fixed them, and most often from store-bought stuff obviously purchased solely for fixing school lunches. There was store bought, soft light bread, Vienna sausage, creme filled cookies, and candy bars. It was rare when I could bring things for lunch attractive enough to trade to these kids, unless they suddenly had a longing for homemade bread.

One of the poorest families had the best trading stuff. They received "commodities", which, for reasons I could never under-

stand, especially at 11:30 in the morning, our family didn't apply
for or qualify. These commodities included canned meat and
fruit. They often brought the best-ever, homemade fried meat
pies and fried fruit pies, especially apricot.

These pies had a folded-over pastry cover crimped at the
edges and were fried in lard or meat drippings. They were chewy
and richly delicious. Thoughts of these pies at 11:30 sometimes
made the morning seem long, and I am sure that schemes for
trading took my mind off my studies. Part of my problem was
that my best traders such as apples and peaches were seasonal,
but commodities were forever.

At the end of the school day when we were walking down the
South Road home, the biscuit and bacon sandwiches weren't too
bad, and we did have hot, buttered homemade bread with jelly,
waiting us at home. The road home always seemed longer than
the road to school. According to Roger Miller, another Oklahoma
product, "It was one mile over and two miles back".

WHO GETS THE BACK OF THE CHICKEN?

Right now, I could not kill a chicken for food, or for almost any other reason. I suppose I could if my children were starving, which they are not; or if I was stranded in the woods for several days and a chicken strolled by. However, in my youth on our dry-land farm, killing animals for food was a way of life, and I accepted it as being necessary. (I have marveled in my later years how we learn to accept situations through experience, changing slowly to be able to commit acts that are, at first, totally unacceptable to us.)

Mom would say, "Go fix dinner; fry a chicken and some spuds, make gravy and get some onions out of the garden". Incidentally, in our part of the country, dinner was taken at noontime, lunch was something you took to school and supper was the last meal of the day. I was the number two child, and my older brother got to work in the fields while I helped mom with the housework.

I caught, wrung, scalded, picked, cut up and fried the chicken. I made white gravy in the drippings, and peeled and fried the potatoes in grease from the drippings can on the back of the stove. I went to the garden for green onions, which I cleaned and stood up in a glass in the middle of the table.

There were seven of us in our family; Mom, Dad and five active, growing children. There were basically seven major parts to a fried chicken; two breasts, two thighs, two legs and one back. (Other parts were usually fried also, such as the neck, giblets, wings and, sometimes, the head and feet). When we all sat down to dinner, the major pieces of chicken came out even. We each had a favorite part, and we finished off the other, less favored parts as the meal went on. I can't remember who preferred dark or light meat, but I do recall that Mom always chose the back.

Years later, my family met at my brother Joe's house in Wichita, Kansas for a family get-together. Mom was living there with Joe at the time. She was about 80 years old, had suffered a stroke and was quite frail. Dad had passed on several years before.

We enjoyed the morning as families such as ours do, mainly catching up on family news, and got ready for dinner. Joe asked Mom if she would like to make some coffee, which she said she would. I watched her carefully measure out the required spoons of ground coffee, look at the amount of coffee she had spooned into the pot and then shake from the can the added amount she thought was needed. I smiled to myself, "Old habits die hard".

The main dish for dinner was fried chicken. As I passed the platter of chicken to Mom, I said that she would be pleased that we had saved her favorite piece, the back, for her. She replied in a soft but certain voice, "I am not going to eat that goddamn back any more".

Mom was always a good, modeling parent.

MEMORIES OF THE WASHITA

In my youth, the Washita Valley consisted of a flat, fertile area along the river, composed of rich soils deposited during occasional flooding. Both sets of my grandparents lived on farms along the Washita, and that is where my parents met, courted and wed.

The Washita River runs about six miles west of Butler, Oklahoma and about the same distance to the east of Hammon. In the1930's, it continued down to the areas of Foss and Clinton. Its tributaries and a network of creeks thread the ranch lands and farmlands of much of western Oklahoma.

I recall family outings, with basket lunches and swinging on a very long rope across a scary swimming hole located in the bend of the river. My dad and other older members of our families would often pull off their shoes and hunt for fish in the pool.

They would move slowly and quietly along the banks with their hands under water searching for catfish that might be resting along the banks and under ledges cut naturally by the flow of the river. Dad said the technique was to sense with your hands along the river banks until you felt a catfish's body, caress the body of the fish and slip your fingers through one its gills' slots. You lost a fish if you flinched. Those of us watching from the safety of the banks gave quiet, moral support for a sudden splashing of the water and a triumphant display of a significant catfish. This means of catching fish was called 'noodling'. When I hear the term or use it, whatever the context, I think of my dad catching fish without hooks or nets or traps on the Washita. "Just noodling around" has always had a special meaning for me.

During the rather dry times in western Oklahoma, the Washita might have seemed rather insignificant. It was quite shallow during the summer months, fed by meager springs upriver. These springs probably had been much more active when the grasses were taller, upland was uncultivated and water seeped into and stayed a while in the ground. The river was muddy and coursing after rains came.

In 1934, a horrifying event took place in the Washita valley. There was an extended series of cloudbursts upstream along the

Washita and in much of its drainage area. There was, also, little to stop the sudden accumulation of water and its rush down the river. A 'headrise' more than 20 feet high came crashing without warning one night down the Washita Valley. We were all stunned by the devastation. Seventeen persons were drowned. Even at my early age, I knew eight of them personally and by name. All five members of the Fenter family were drowned. Of seven members of the Bush family, the parents and one daughter were drowned. Three sons of the Bush family survived after heroic efforts to save one another and the rest of their family members. One son was away from home at the time of the flood.

After the water had subsided, our family drove out to the river. My most vivid visual memory was that of a dead horse and a cow caught 20 feet in the air among the branches of the huge cottonwood trees. I will never forget my bewilderment at the loss of persons I knew, many of them my good friends. This world was a mass of mud, with drifts of branches, furniture, clothing and pieces of homes.

During those times, we all sought entertainment and distraction to ease the despair that beset us, which also included the effects of a dustbowl and a worldwide depression. As an example, the merchants of Butler provided a competitive talent show each Saturday night during the Summer. They placed a flatbed truck in the middle of main street, and anyone who could sing, tell stories, dance or play instruments was encouraged to participate. The prize for first place was $10, a considerable sum in those days.

Soon after the flood, a young man called "Crazy" Elkins appeared on the show accompanied by a guitarist. For three weeks running he won first place with a song he had written about the Washita Valley flood. He had the full attention and the tears of most of the Butler community. Sixty years later, I found that his given name was "Baze" and that he lived with his family in the Washita valley area. Rumor had it that he went crazy after the rejection of a favorite girl friend. He was also known as a brilliant, creative young man.

I remember, yet, parts of the song and its haunting melody:

"When above the town of Hammon, Heavy rain and hail came down.
For hours the maddening cloudbursts Came pouring to the ground.
The streams that joined the Washita Were swelled like narrow lakes,
And merging with the river
Spread sorrow in their wake."

I have tried without success to find the full copy of the song. I grew up listening to the songs of the Carter Family, Jimmy Rodgers and the Arkansas Woodchopper, and later to Woody Guthrie, Pete Seeger, Hank Williams, Bob Dylan and the Beatles. I have always thought Crazy Elkins' "Washita Valley Flood" ranked among the songs of these recognized writers and performers. He had a good voice and a good heart, splitting his $10 best performance award down the middle with his guitarist (Who, I found out just recently, was also his brother).

The Washita is different now. Fortunately there should be no more catastrophic floods, what with weather warning systems, farm ponds, terraces, flood control dams and the Foss Reservoir. The reservoir extends north to Highway 33. It covers many of the old valley farms, but provides welcome recreational opportunities and even wetlands as the droughts dictate the flow of the river and the level of water in the reservoir.

My memories of the Washita River, happy and sad, are set. Many things now associated with the river are new, but do not replace my memories of friends lost in the flood and of Crazy Elkins and of Dad noodling for catfish.

Footnote: Special thanks go to Ed Covey, now one of the area's County Commissioners, whose interests in the Washita Valley flood are as passionate as mine, and whose memories are equally vivid. This account was based mainly on my recollections as a twelve year old boy, with Ed providing corroborating and correcting information.

SWEEPING THE BACK YARD

The Tusing family lived about three-quarters of a mile south of us, up a hill and around a bend. Their farm was much like ours, upland mostly, with red thin soil, which never should have been plowed but left to buffalo grass. The Tusings, as did we, eked out a living on their dry land farm, growing livestock, meager cash crops, fruit and vegetables for basic sustenance. This was a harsh land and a harsh climate, but it was home.

The Tusings had twin daughters, Essie and Jessie, and a son named Clyde. I don't remember too much about the daughters but I recall parts of Clyde's life with great clarity and joy. Clyde was tall, quick and strong and a great athlete. I am sure he would have been a rich and famous baseball player had he been born 50 years later.

Mrs. Tusing was short and round and one for long, casual conversations. Mom would sometimes send me up to Mrs. Tusing's to deliver or borrow something, often yeast starter for sourdough bread. Mrs. Tusing and Mom both made great bread, and both served it hot with butter and jelly. I didn't mind the long walk or pony ride to Mrs. Tusing's place or back home, anticipating the goodies at both ends of the journey.

I remember well their house and yard. The back yard didn't sprout one blade of grass. Their well water was pumped by a windmill located down the slope from the house and was used for watering livestock. It was far too gyppy for cooking or for continued use in growing plants. Rainwater collected from the roof of the house and stored in cisterns was prized for cooking, washing hair and making coffee. In those dry days, if fresh water was available it, for sure, wasn't used to nurture the grass in the back yard.

Mrs. Tusing didn't mind the bare yard; in fact, it seemed to provide a great deal of satisfaction for her. She swept it with her house broom and spread the debris and chicken poop on her small, very efficient garden and flowers. Her yard was immaculate. We would often sit on her back porch, talking about our families and other pertinent topics, more than comfortable with the view.

The Tusings sold their farm when I was a teenager and moved to town. Their new house was on the way into town for us, and I would visit with Mrs. Tusing now and then. During the summer and fall months I would peddle garden stuff, mainly roasting ears, cucumbers and cantaloupe, from gunnysacks hanging from the horn of the saddle on our old pony. It was always good to stop by Mrs. Tusing's to try to get her to buy some stuff and to visit a while.

They had moved into a neat white bungalow with a picket fence around it. There was city water, and they used it to grow a green, well-tended lawn, which gave Mr. Tusing a great deal of pride. Although Mrs. Tusing was careful not to complain to him about their new place, she told me privately that she missed being able to sweep her back yard. But, as always, she was ready with the warm, buttered sourdough bread, with jelly.

THE STANLEY PLAYERS COME TO BUTLER

Each summer of the 1930's the Stanley Players brought their traveling theater to Butler. They set up a big tent in a vacant lot on main street just south of Word's Grocery Store.

This event generated considerable excitement in Butler and its farm community, in part because it was live theater and in part because of the people who made up the Stanley Players. Mr. and Mrs. Stanley headed up the show along with their son, John. I don't recall the names of the other people in the touring group, but they seemed to be part of an extended Stanley family.

The Stanley Players would stay for an entire week, preparing for shows to be presented during midweek and the weekend. We locals found that show people were real people, and there was a general feeling of trust and pleasure going both ways between the players and the members of our community. Seeing one of them in the local drugstore brought considerable curiosity and satisfaction to us all. We were amazed how different performers looked without their makeup.

The Stanley cast presented a different play each night, ranging from light comedies of the "Toby" series, to melodrama and dark mystery. Often the cast would include local people who could fit a part in a play and could learn lines quickly. One of our prettiest Butler girls, Lois Ashley, often got parts. The young men of Butler had mixed feelings because Lois was usually cast as the object of affection of one of the younger male Stanley players. Pride in Lois and jealousy ran neck and neck, so to speak. The usual male lead was John Stanley, a

tall, dark haired young man, considered to be quite handsome by Butler standards. The plays were done well, and the performances were sincerely appreciated by their audiences. There were also between act presentations, balanced between pure huckstering and olio. The cast members would work the audience to sell boxes of candy which contained slips of paper denoting prizes that could be redeemed on stage at that moment.

There were intermission performances by cast members, which were quite good. John Stanley had an excellent voice and a great stage presence. He would sing funny, catchy songs and then lead the audience in well taught choruses. One favorite of mine was "Grandma's Lye Soap". He would bang out the rhythm with a folded newspaper and sing,

"Mrs. O'Malley, down in the valley,
Had some ulcers, I understand,
Then she ate some of Grandma's lye soap
And has the cleanest ulcers in the land...
Now, sing it right out for Grandma's lye soap..."

John later performed bit parts in Hollywood, and I recall hearing the strains of "Grandma's Lye Soap" on the radio. We were beset by a depression and dustbowl and an impending war that took much of our immediate attention; consequently we tended not to follow transient affairs too closely, but his world was a part of ours for one week of each year.

After the Stanley family struck its tent and left town, probably to Hammon to the west, life seemed quiet in our farm community, as though a tornado had passed through with an accompanying beneficial rain for the crops.

MY FATHER'S SONGS

My father, to my knowledge, never bowed his head for any one, even God. I never thought of it as arrogance, but that he thought of it as unnecessary. I never heard him pray publicly, which I thought, from my reading the Bible about ostentation in this area, would be quite acceptable to God. When Dad was asked to lead in prayer in church or to return thanks before a meal, he gave a quiet, "Please excuse me". I never felt embarrassed or had concern for him in these situations.

We went to church regularly. The programs always included singing; in fact, some of them were made up of only singing.

Dad really wanted us to go to church, and he shepherded us through our getting ready and arriving there on time. He always sang in the choir, and he always sang bass. He had an acceptable singing voice, especially if the bass notes were limited to about a three-note range. He was fearless. He would take the long bass lead in the chorus of "Church in the Valley" with strength and great enthusiasm. He sang "Power in the Blood" admirably, even if no other bases were there to protect him. We all knew why Dad liked to go to church.

Dad wanted us to have a family quartet, and we really tried. My brother Joe was a most reluctant tenor; Mom sang a respectable alto; I followed more than led in the lead spot; my sister Mary played good tent-revival piano and Dad provided impetus with his ready bass voice and his insistence that we perform as a family group. He was immensely proud of us. I really don't know if we were very good, but, as I recall, we were not asked to perform a lot.

I would not presume to know Dad's life in the hereafter. If he landed in heaven, the herald angels and the heavenly choir might pick up an enthusiastic, though irreverent bass singer. Their music would have added fervor and, within certain ranges, a welcome amount of harmony.

WORSHIPPING WITH BYNA AND JESSIE

Church for our community was held in the wooden two-room school building located six miles north of Butler. The community, the school and church were all called New Home.

Sunday school and church were held regularly; at least, Sunday school was. Church followed Sunday school when a preacher was available. There were no preachers living in the community; consequently, the availability of a preacher depended on several factors, including the weather. We always had Sunday school; at the end of each service, the Sunday school superintendent would announce, "We will all meet here next Sunday morning, God willing and if the creeks don't rise".

During my preadolescent years, I found a confusing number of things to like and not to like about my religious beginnings and church. I felt good about the singing, seeing my friends and neighbors, the socials held by the church, the involvement of my entire family in going to church and Sunday school and, at times, a certain amount of security.

What I did not like was the testimonial service, the invitation to salvation and a growing feeling that the motivation for religious involvement was fear of dying, not love of God. I also did not like Byna Wright and Jessie Frazier chasing after me.

The testimonial service began with the Sunday School Superintendent asking, "Now, who will be first to testify?" Most adults would rise and tell about the joys of their religion. One could also simply stand and give a bible verse, which many of the younger ones would do. Shy ones would often quote "Jesus wept". If one wanted to use an easily remembered verse, he needed to be the first to give it; consequently, some of the younger ones were prompted to present themselves early in this part of the program. The beatitudes came in handy; with "Blessed are the meek for they shall inherit the earth" being a popular choice, although it didn't always seem to fit the general tenor of the community. A real challenge was "For God so loved the world he gave his own begotten son that whosoever believeth in him would have everlasting life". This last one seemed to be a real crowd pleaser among the adults, seeing their nods and smiles. I felt their reaction confirmed the reason they came to church.

A second painful part would come for me if I delayed testifying until the end - or did not participate at all. There would be an embarrassing pause after the superintendent called out, "Is there anyone else who would like to testify for Jesus?" I felt the eyes of the world were on me - that the superintendent might as well have called out my name.

The 'age of accountability' for both boys and girls was twelve years. If you died before that age, your soul, through innocence, was bound for heaven. If you were 12 years old, you were accountable for your sins, and if you had not been saved by the blood of Christ, you were bound for Hell. Being saved, ironically, was a traumatic, fearful time for me.

On the surface, the process of being saved was quite simple. At the end of the church service, the choir would sing a 'song of invitation'; the preacher would ask anyone who wanted to be saved to come forward to the prayer bench in front of him. The supplicant would come forward, kneel at the bench, confess his sins to Christ and ask for forgiveness. When the sinner indicated that forgiveness had been received, he or she would turn to the congregation, admit their sins and state that Christ had forgiven all of them.

For me, the process was far from simple. It was a psychological horror. I dreaded the choir's rendering a woeful, plaintive song to begin the invitation session. Their selections included such songs as 'Oh, Why Not Tonight?', 'Jesus Keep Me Near the Cross' and 'Nearer my God to Thee'. I often thought of the Titanic, which had sunk some 20 years earlier, identifying quite closely with it as it slid under the waves.

The preacher would give the invitation for sinners to come forward. He began by talking about the joys of salvation, hold out his arms and say, "Sinners, won't you come?" If no one responded, the positive approach often gave way to warnings about dying unsaved and subsequently going to hell. He would remind the sinners they may not have another chance, that they may not live until the next invitation was offered; they might die tonight or on the way home or when it was least expected. One of the preachers would talk about the frailness of human life, using such expressions as "For you, there may be a snapping of the brickle thread of life". He was a very passionate, but uneducated man, and replacing 'brittle' with 'brickle' was all the same to him. It did detract from his message, however, and made me wonder about the reliability of the whole salvation process.

Everyone in the congregation knew the identity of those who had not been saved. Some of the older persons really worried about them and volunteered to help the preacher out. Two of the women who were most concerned about others' salvation were Byna Wright and Jessie Frazier. At least, I assumed that was the motivation for their actions. These were two wonderful women for whom I had a lot of respect. If no one responded to the preacher, they would take it on themselves to approach the sinners and try to convince them that they should come up to the altar. I hated to see the lack of response from others, especially when I saw Byna or Jessie heading in my direction.

What changing roles for Byna and Jessie from the way I knew them outside the church! I thought of them as mothers of my best friends, as laughing providers of food at school or church socials, or as persons canning food with Mom, even laughing uproariously at a risqué joke or comment. I wasn't prepared for the looks on their lined faces then as they implored me to be saved. They offered to hold my hand as I would walk to the bench, and gave it a suggestive initial tug. I resisted for some time, not because of lack of belief, but the fear of appearing in front of all those people far exceeded any fears I might have had of spending an eternity in hell. I felt guilty when they and the preacher gave up for the day, but that was balanced fairly by my immediate, though temporary, sense of relief.

One night after I had gone to bed, I overheard Mom tell Dad that she was worried about me, what with my being over 12 years old and not being saved yet. Dad's silence may have been his comment. I never asked Dad's advice in the matter, knowing he would recommend a pragmatic, rather than religious, response.

I received salvation the very next Sunday. It was a tough week as I wondered if I would live that long and dreading the first step toward the front of the church. Part of my capitulation was not to disappoint Mom, as I had a feeling that she would worry and feel guilty for the rest of her life if I died unrepentant. The next week as the preacher first began the invitation; I started walking toward him, alone. I had decided it would be easier to start at

the sound of the gun. I was numb with fear, and I felt most con-
spicuous. I was relieved to kneel at the bench, where I could feel
that I didn't fill the entire front of the church - and where I could
be alone.

   But not for long. Byna and Jessie joined me, hugging me and
asking the Lord to forgive me of my sins. As I recall, several other
members joined us, either to help out or, perhaps, to keep me
from bolting the scene. After a while, the preacher placed his
hand on my shoulder and, addressing me as 'Brother Roger',
asked if I had confessed my sins to God. I nodded yes and did
not speak. Then he asked if I thought He had forgiven all my
sins, to which I obviously gave a numb, affirmative sign.

   I knew that despite the horrific, past few minutes, the worst
was yet to come. The preacher told me to turn around and face
the congregation and to tell them that I had been a sinner but
that I believed the Lord had forgiven all my sins. I haven't the
foggiest recollection of what I surely mumbled to the audience,
but it was enough.

   I recall feeling relieved in the days following my being saved.
I'm not sure why. Perhaps it was because Mom seemed happy for
me; perhaps it was that I thought heaven was worth it all or, perhaps, that I could now enjoy the invitation ceremony without
Byna and Jessie being after me.

   In later years, I learned that my Catholic friends had enjoyed
the luxury of a private confession to the priest, and, also, that
God wasn't big on public prayer or lamentations. I have wondered if this traumatic episode had not given me my continued
fear of public speaking, rather than its having been caused by the
long hours of solitude in the fields talking only to the horses.

   Then I was baptized. At the New Home Church, new members were baptized any place there was a sufficient depth of
water, usually in a creek. At that time, there were no lakes in our
area, and farm ponds for conservation purposes were a few years
down the road. I was baptized in our swimming hole, a deep
part of the creek that divided our property from Jack Wright's
farm. It felt strange, skinny-dipping in the hole all week and then
going into the water with my clothes on the next Sunday.

   The preacher would stand in the water about waist deep,
hold out his hand and guide the subject into position in front of
him. He'd say quietly, "Hold your nose and trust me". He would

then intone for all to hear, "And now I baptize thee in the name of the Father and of the Son and of the Holy Ghost". Many of the people who were baptized into our church had not been around water very much, could not swim and were terrified at the thought of being submerged, especially face up. Being baptized, for them, took a real leap of faith in God ... and in the preacher.

I have always appreciated the convenience that other denominations enjoy with 'sprinkling baptisms'. But rituals are rituals, and one could hardly have his sins 'washed away' with a mere sprinkling. One of our preachers smugly told the tale of a man about to be baptized by sprinkling who asked the preacher, "But how are you going to get me to fit in that little cup?"

As time went on, I slowly moved away from any organized church. At times, I feel a loss, knowing that I could make church work for me, especially in the right church. When I am asked if I am religious, I honestly say, "Yes". The tenets of my personal religion, however, are quite different from those proposed for my early training - and far less numerous. These are that one should stand strong on freedom of religion for all persons, demonstrate one's beliefs through just treatment of all living things and, finally, not worry about the hereafter, but appreciate the gift of life on earth. I do, in honesty and modesty, however, recognize that there is a power greater than human kind and, most certainly, greater than I.

HOWENSTINES AND FOURACRES

The Butler Bank was located in a two-story brick building at the intersection of the main streets in Butler, Oklahoma. It had an imposing front entrance with inlaid tile on the front landing and an impressive pillar supporting the part of the building overhanging the landing. At the rear of the building, a set of iron stairs led to the outside door on the second floor.

The building was obviously constructed originally to be a bank. It looked like a bank. The teller counter was made of stone materials, and a set of bars separated customers from the tellers. The experience of going into the bank was overwhelming for me as a boy.

Dolph Howenstine, the bank president, was tall, dark and austere. He talked with people in his office at the front of the building behind a low partition. I often wondered why he didn't talk with them in a more private place, since their discussions were probably about money matters, which, it seemed to me, should be private.

Mrs. Howenstine was the main teller. She was a formidable to me as was her husband. Rather short in stature, she was also short of tongue. She used a lot of makeup which I thought to be intended to affect her position of distance and authority, and she seemed to run her part of the bank with full efficiency and totally without humor.

I didn't have occasion to go into the bank very often as a youngster, usually only after being excused for a short period at school to do necessary business for my dad. I recall one occasion of being sent to the bank by Mrs. Hackworth, my English teacher and class sponsor, to obtain coins for the cash box for the Senior Play. Giving my handful of bills to Mrs. Howenstine, I explained what we needed in coins. She started by pushing out a stack of dimes, saying "Here is a dollar in dimes". I thought she said, "Here is a dollar and a dime". I timidly called her on the discrepancy. Fortunately I have forgotten her response, but I was totally devastated. My recalling such a minor incident tells me she was impressive, and that I was impressionable. Despite the formidable air of Mr. and Mrs. Howenstine, I have always suspected a latent generosity behind those unsmiling faces. Mrs. Fouracres and her son lived above the bank. I didn't know either of them well, and my impressions of them are those of a youngster growing up on a farm 4 1/2 miles out of town. The Fouracres used the stairs at the back of the bank to enter their part of the building. Mrs. Fouracres was a quiet, dowdy, unkempt woman who gave doting, constant care to her severely retarded teenage son. No one seemed to know where they came from. One of my memories of them was their climbing the iron stairs together, both awkwardly. Another, their picking lambsquarter, wild careless weed good for greens in its early stages, along the banks of the road. Lambsquarter greens was a staple for many families, being served as a vegetable, and canned for winter use.

I have always wondered at the relationships between the Howenstine and the Fouracres. Knowing the Howenstines to be relatively wealthy and the Fouracres to be poor, their connection was surely the benevolence extended by the bankers. There were few organized programs at that time to give non-governmental aid to the poor. Assistance from individuals was extended specifically, privately, and with extreme consideration for pride of the individual persons, whether they be the giver or the recipient.

I often wondered if the Fouracres had electric lights and gas heat as did the first floor of the bank, luxuries denied farm folk in those days. Did the Fouracres clean the bank for their rent? Did they somehow pay for their rent? Did the Howenstines provide these amenities gratuitously? These questions are moot now. The main thing for me is that both the Fouracres and the Howenstines lived through the same hard times, though at significantly different levels. I like to think the Howenstines showed grace to the Fouracres and that it was returned in full measure.

Sadly, the Fouracres boy died one day falling down the metal stairs. At his funeral, well attended by local community members, Mrs. Fouracres sobbed uncontrollably, saying that she was happy her son was gone, knowing he wouldn't be hungry any more in heaven.

The reactions of the community to the mother of the Fouracres boy were kind and generous. The support of the Howenstines still remains a mystery to me. This may have been Butler's way of providing for the homeless.

WATERMELON PETE

One of my many pleasures is eating watermelon, and much of my joy must surely be linked to the pleasant memories of my farm childhood and youth. Watermelon, with its texture, its sweetness, its juice tastes as good to me now as it did when I was growing up on the farm. Not so other childhood pleasures such as cotton candy and candy hearts or smoking corn silks and grapevines.

In one of the ultimate practices of diversified farming, Dad planted rows of watermelon, muskmelon and black-eyed peas among the rows of cotton. The joys of taking melons to the house for breakfast or a treat in the hot afternoon were memorable.

In the Fall after frost had come, the melons tasted even better. When we were picking cotton, the melons were nearby for a welcome break. I often wondered if Dad hadn't planned this juxtaposition as an incentive for us to pick cotton. One of the negatives about eating watermelons in the field was that you had no easy way to wash the juice from your arms as it ran down wrists and dripped from elbows.

Along with the delicious memories of eating watermelons are the recollections of the fun associated with this succulent fruit. In addition to the joys of eating watermelon at almost any country occasion, it provided other equally delightful activities. I recall our neighbor, "Grandpa" Wright ambling down the road and saying without ceremony, "Let's get a watermelon". He lived with his son Jack's family a quarter of a mile north of us. Everyone knew him as "Grandpa"; it mattered not whether he was a blood relative.

One of us would go out to the field and pull one of our best melons, and we would eat it, usually in the back yard. I recall that Grandpa would eat his share of the melon but never spit out any seeds until he was finished, and then not until he began his trek back home. Then he would blow them out of his mouth systematically. We wondered first of all how he did it, and then why he waited so long. Was he being polite and mannerly, or just showing off?

If we didn't have an acceptable melon in our field or garden, we slipped into Hubert Lee's patch to get one. Hubert, Ethel and their daughter, LaVena, lived about an eighth of a mile north of us on the other side of the road. He raised great watermelons along the creek bottom, especially the yellow-meated kind.

At the time of my youth, stealing was an absolute no. It was the most reprehensible of sins. That is, except for watermelons. This exception provided numerous opportunities for excitement and fun, including such antics as our lifting up the rear end of the town night watchman's Model A Ford, placing the rear wheels in fresh watermelon rinds and covertly watching him try to pull out from the curb.

Weekend forays by our teenage "gang" to steal watermelons were done with careful planning and a certain amount of daring. We learned where the best patches were and the quickest, safest way to access each patch and get away with some rather heavy watermelons. There were three unspoken rules: don't destroy the host's other property; never bust a melon in the field; and don't get caught. Our two best targets were Alva Cole's farm on Barnitz Creek, and the patch of Hubert Lee.

I stole a lot of watermelons from Hubert, and as I found out, he was aware of it. One day, we were eating a yellow-meated melon in our driveway when he came by, and I had a strong feeling he knew where I had obtained it.

Hubert started calling me "Watermelon Pete" as an initial greeting when he drove by our place or saw me in town. I was somehow pleased, in part for the recognition and, more so, for the implication he didn't take my transgressions too seriously. It was especially pleasing for me to hear, "Hey, Watermelon Pete" when I came home from the Navy and, later, from a teaching job. It was a bit of home.

Years later, I moved to Denver to accept a position with the Department of Education. I bought an acreage in one of the suburbs, and I took great pleasure in growing a large garden, which included a variety of melons. I found that watermelons don't grow as well in Denver as they do in Oklahoma.

One day I was working in the garden in the front yard when I was shaken by a shout from the street, "Hey, Watermelon Pete". In the car stopped in the front of the house were Hubert, Ethel and LaVena.

I found to my joy that Hubert and Ethel owned an apartment house in Lafayette, a small town just to the north and west of Denver, and LaVena was a home economics teacher in one of the local schools. I was wistful I didn't have ripe watermelons to help repay my rightful debts to Hubert. It would have been most fitting. Even so, my heart swelled with a familiar boyhood pleasure to be hailed once more as "Watermelon Pete".

MRS. HACKWORTH

Mrs. Helen Hackworth came out to Butler, Oklahoma to teach high school English in 1938. Butler had a population of about 400 then, and students came from both the town and the surrounding farm community. The school enrolled about 250 grade and high school students; my graduating class numbered just 11 students.

The dustbowl was mainly over, although its effects were still being felt, not by only the farmers but by all persons living in our area. There was little greenery and little natural beauty based on current botanical standards. The depression was still in control, although things were getting to be a bit better in that grown men could make two bucks a day instead of one.

As a student, I wondered why such a classy lady would come to teach school in such a setting. Later, I realized that this was probably a choice she made based on the economic pressures of the time, certainly not on the joys of living in Butler. Incidentally, I doubt she had indoor plumbing in Butler; I recall only the banker and doctor did in those days.

She taught us Shakespeare, reading much of it with us and to us, explaining its meaning and making us memorize many of the parts that were related to our lives. She taught us to diagram sentences, teaching us inductively (as I learned later) about subjects, verbs, objects of verbs, nominative case and agreement of subjects and verbs in a variety of ways.

Mrs. Hackworth was austere in her appearance and her demeanor. I realize now that she relished her role as an adult and carried out this role as a surrogate, caring parent by the book, as it were. She had no children of her own, but I'll bet she would have been a wonderful, scary parent. I have a feeling she really enjoyed being our teacher.

As I look back on my high school days and my time with Mrs. Hackworth, I am amazed at her teaching skills and her ability to work with the young people of the Butler community. She understood who we were and what was important to us.

High school basketball was important to Butler High School, to the Butler community and to me. I am sure that adolescent peer attitudes had a lot to do with my wanting to be on the basketball team. There was little else to do except to go home to the farm.

Basketball practice was held during the last school period. Afterward, I had to hustle to shower and dress to catch the bus home. When I stayed to shoot baskets or dawdled with my friends and missed the bus, I walked four and one-half miles home.

Mrs. Hackworth knew how much basketball meant to me. She and I both knew that I was not a great player, but good enough to make the Butler team. She was not above using my wanting to play ball as barter to make me do better in my classwork. If I was not a hotshot basketball player, I was an even worse literature student.

We studied literature for 12 weeks each semester, followed by grammar for six weeks. I flunked literature for one period, and Mrs. Hackworth laid down the law that I had to make an A in grammar or fail the course. If I failed the course I couldn't play ball, so she said. I don't know where she got that authority. I just knew she could do it.

She supported my flailing away in grammar by giving me a paperback copy of Walsh's Handbook of English Usage, which I was to memorize, so she also said. I couldn't understand why I should know about reflexive usage, ablatives and that "none" was singular, but I did know that I wanted to be on the basketball team.

Later, I went off to Southwestern State College at my mother's insistence, to study to be a civil engineer, although I had no idea what such a person did to make a living. Entering freshmen were given an entrance examination in English usage, taken verbatim, I swear, from some of the exercises in Walsh's handbook. I should have made a perfect score, but I was good enough to get my picture in the college newspaper. The picture should have been of Mrs. Hackworth or of Walsh or Mom.

Incidentally, I can still recite the last stanza of William Cullen Bryant's "Thanatopsis" and many of the pithy lines from "MacBeth". Coincidentally, I never made the Butler Herald on my basketball scores, even though my Uncle Grady was the editor.

DIAGRAMMING SENTENCES
(Dinking around with usage)

Memory is the most forgiving of all our faculties. We remember good times and repress bad ones. Sentence diagramming in Mrs. Hackworth's high school English classes I remember. We filled the chalkboards with words and lines, and, incidentally, learned something about sentence structure
.   I don't want to get into an argument on curriculum here, but I have won a few parlor bets about use of words by placing them in perspective with diagrams. What follows is based on a dim recollection of my labors in classes in high school English taught by Mrs. Hackworth in 1938 at Butler, Oklahoma. She was a masterful teacher. I will be remiss, as she would no doubt say, if I do not go to the library to check out the accuracy of my memories.

The following examples of diagramming are restricted to simple sentences, partly because my memories of complex and compound sentences are dimmer yet. Hopefully they also will bring painless memories to the reader.

(1) The boy sweats.

boy	sweats
The	

This is a simple sentence with an intransitive verb. Separate the subject (in this case a noun) and predicate (the verb) with an extended vertical line.

(2) The nervous boy sweats profusely.

boy	sweats
The	profusely
nervous	

Adjectives and adverbs are modifiers.

(3) Mommy rocks the baby's cradle slowly.

Mommy	rocks	cradle
	slowly	the
		baby's

"Rocks" is a transitive verb; "cradle" is the object of the verb.
Note the short vertical line between the verb and its object.

(4) Tom is tall.

"Tall" is an adjective and reflects back to the subject to modify or
describe it. It is in the nominative case. Note the slanted line following the verb, rather than the upright one in the preceding
example, which denotes objective case.

(5) Dick runs very fast.

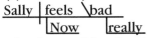

Adverbs modify verbs and adverbs.

(6) Sally often feels bad.

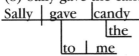

"bad" is an adjective referring back to the subject.

(7) Now Sally feels really bad.

Sally | feels \bad
        |Now |really

Adverbs modify adjectives also.

(8) Sally gave the candy to me.

Sally | gave |candy
               |the
       |to | me

"me" is the object of the preposition "to", and the prepositional
phrase modifies the verb. Is this fun, or what? If you want a real
challenge, diagram the Preamble to the Constitution (after a visit
to the library). Try complex sentences with both adverbial and
adjectival clauses; compound sentences will compound the fun. I
often wish Mrs. Hackworth were here (Or is it "was here"?).

THE PRIDE OF THE COUNTY

There was considerable interest in athletics in rural areas in the 1930s and 40s. However, because of poor roads, economics and a lack of organization that arranged state or national championships, competition in team sports was limited to local areas. As a result, many excellent athletes were unknown outside individual counties and had little opportunity to play in the big time.

One cannot help but wonder how the lives of some young people who had great athletic ability might have been changed by having the opportunity to play before a national or international audience. Several persons come to mind. Clyde Tusing lived three-quarters of a mile south of us on a farm as poor as ours. He was tall, wiry and quick. My first knowledge of Clyde's athletic skills was watching him play on the Butler men's baseball team.

Baseball games were played with other local area teams on Saturdays or Sundays. There were neither uniforms nor baseball shoes. The usual attire was bib overalls and work shoes. Although there was no admission charge, a hat was always passed around among the spectators to pay for the balls and, hopefully, some bats. Games were played on the local high school field or in a local pasture. The sole, unpaid umpire stood behind the pitcher, and was appreciated by most of the spectators because they had somehow escaped this thankless chore. Playing conditions were not optimal.

Clyde played center field. I was amazed how quickly he could move with long, loping strides to catch fly balls or to return ground balls, and how unerring were his throws to the infield.

Clyde made his own bat out of a willow tree limb, and when he hit a pitched ball the sound cracked sharp and loud. There were no ball park fences, and consequently many of the balls he hit were never found, much to the consternation of fans and the other players at the necessary delay of the game resulting from the search for the ball.

On one Fourth of July in the mid thirties, the Butler community held an outing on one of the town's vacant lots. There was the usual potluck and watermelon and a baseball game between the Butler team and the Hammon Indian team, made up of native Americans. Their pitcher, a slender handsome young man, had one of smoothest deliveries I had ever seen and a very confusing curve ball. I did not know his name; "Feather Fingers" would have been most fitting. I recall that the Hammon team won the game. However, my most vivid memory of the celebration was a foot race before the game between Clyde Tusing and a fellow named Jarnigan (His first name escapes me).

The Jarnigan family had moved to the Butler area from one of the larger cities and lived in one of the unused farmhouses. I knew little about them, except they had glass covered bookcases filled with many beautiful books. Jarnigan was a young fellow, not too tall, and I thought him to be, at that time, somewhat 'cocky'.

I don't recall what prompted this matched race. Clyde and Jarnigan lived within a mile of one another and may have set the race themselves. I suspect there may have been several wagers on the outcome of the race.

The distance set for the race was 100 yards. Jarnigan appeared at the starting line wearing running shorts and track spikes. I had never seen track spikes before, and I was impressed with the shiny needles and how lightweight the shoes appeared to be. Clyde arrived wearing overalls and work shoes. I recall feeling concern for Clyde with his obvious disadvantages in the race. The contrasts were made more apparent by Clyde's height of 6'2" and Jarnigan at a compact 5'7".

At the beginning of the race, Jarnigan was well in front, but as the race progressed, Clyde came alongside. I was surprised to note their heads seemed to be at the same level, no doubt because of Clyde's stride. Clyde then won the race by an unquestioned margin.

I have often wondered if, given the opportunity, Clyde might have changed some of the recorded results in the Olympic Games, or whether he might have been loping around the New York Yankee outfield, much to the adulation of a young Joe DiMaggio.

James Collins lived on a farm in the Washita valley and attended a small high school called Pie Flat. The school was located about half way between Butler and Hammon. Our boys basketball team played theirs regularly, and all too often for our happiness and well being.

James was an absolute terror as a basketball player. He was taller than any of our players, and he seemed even taller when the game began. He was muscular, and he could jump far above anyone else. He dominated the game on either end of the court, and when the ball was in his hands there was no way of stopping him from scoring. He asserted himself constantly, and he had no compunction against bruising his opponent's body or ego. James provided leadership and support for his teammates and the nucleus for scoring and defense. During his senior year, James led his team into the Oklahoma State High School Basketball tournament.

After being graduated from high school and completing military service, James chose to stay in the area and to continue farming. Had he wished to pursue a career in basketball, and had opportunities to move into the profession, I believe he would have made a great power forward or a most powerful guard. I was nearly overcome with joy and relief when he was graduated from high school and became just another interested spectator at our games.

Ed Whiteskunk played in the guard position on Hammon's high school basketball team. He was several years older than I was and I never had the pleasure of playing with or against him. But I watched him play on several occasions. He was a cool character; setting up the plays and helping the team execute them. I was amazed at the skills he had in passing the ball to other players. The opposing players never intercepted his passes; no one knew where the ball was going, except for the Hammon players. He looked one way and passed the other. He had an uncanny sense of ways to move to a seeming special place on the court and to score. When Ed played, basketball seemed magical.

Ed was Native American. There were many Native Americans living in the Hammon area, most of them from Plains Tribes. On occasion I went with my Dad to buy cattle from them from time to time. I remember meeting a beautiful, dignified older man, grey hair in braids. Dad called him 'Sox', and I never questioned whether this was an English or a tribal name. It was always spoken with great respect.

I have often wondered how Ed would have fared in professional basketball, as I have wondered about the young pitcher,

"Feather Fingers", on the Hammon men's baseball team.

Finally, my thoughts turn to my youngest brother, J.T., and what he might have done in the professional baseball world with proper coaching, visits to tryout camps and being seen by team scouts. What intrigued me about the potential for his being a professional was his likeness to Babe Ruth. As a high school player he played various positions as was needed for the team. He was, as was Ruth, an acceptable pitcher with good speed and an unstable knuckleball that left bruises all over the catcher and the batters befuddled. He was also a good catcher and first baseman, but, like Ruth, wasn't a terror on the basepaths. He would have been the spitting image of Babe Ruth had his tummy been a bit bigger.

J.T.'s main strengths lay in his ability to hit the ball a country mile and in his enduring spirit. He was, and is, a burly guy with unneeded extra strength in his upper torso, and a great quickness in his hands. He still has phenomenal eyesight. It was always comforting to have him come to bat in a critical situation of a game.

I have included J.T. in this list of deserving but undiscovered athletes for four good reasons. One, because of his early athletic attributes; two, because he didn't have the opportunity to develop further his potential as a player; three, he is my brother; and four, because I was his coach during his senior year of high school. I feel remiss in not having known enough to give him the opportunity to go to the Big Apple as a recognized athlete.

And what about Clyde, James, Ed and Feather Fingers?

PARTY LINES

Telephones were an essential part of our lives as farmers in the 30s and 40s. When we heard the telephone ring a short sound, then a long sound and then another short one, we knew the call was for our house.

Our telephone was encased in a solid oak box on the south wall of the living room. The receiver was on the left side cradled in a metal lever, the mouthpiece was on the front of the phone box and could be adjusted for the height of the speaker, and the crank for ringing another number was on the right side of the box.

Our phone number was listed in the telephone book as 20-151. This meant we were on line number 20, and our ring was "a short, a long and a short". Mrs.Tusing's number was something like 20-25, two shorts and a long. If we were out in the yard and the phone rang, the usual question to one another was "Was that our number?"

If I wanted to talk to Mrs. Tusing I cranked, as best I could, two shorts and a long. Quite naturally, Grandpa Wright, Hubert Lee and Minnie Nye, all on line 20 could listen also if they chose to do so. Conscience said that one shouldn't listen in; curiosity said "Why not?" There was a certain loss of privacy on the party line. I don't recall how many phones were on line 20; there were often several clicks in my ear when I made or received a call. One was spared the sounds of heavy breathing since the mouthpiece and the receiver were separated on the telephone boxes.

If I wanted to talk to J.R. Bibb, I cranked one long ring for the central operator, and asked for a number such as 16-152. The central operator was usually Mrs. Noel. She and her husband, Ray, were the Butler telephone company. She ran the switch-board, and Ray took care of the lines and the equipment. Since all of us need to sleep sometimes, telephone service didn't exist during the night; although I could call Mrs. Tusing and other persons on line 20.

There were several advantages to being on a party line. For one, you were privy to a considerable amount of information. In addition to eavesdropping, you could be informed of major

events by the central operator making a "general" call, preceded
by a series of long rings and announcing such things as the clos-
ing of schools because of bad weather, the approach of a tornado
to your area, or upcoming special events. An additional service
from Mrs. Noel was her gratuitous information, that the person
you were trying to call had gone to Clinton to buy school
clothes.

There were, naturally, downsides to the party line in addition
to the loss of privacy and the lack of service at night. One main
concern was the sharing of time with other subscribers to line
20. The usual general question posed when the receiver was lifted in preparation to call someone was "Is the line busy?"

Dad was not long on casual conversation whether or not he
was on the phone. He didn't talk over the phone too much and
used it mainly to talk with someone about buying livestock. Even
then, his conversations were short and to the point. However,
Minnie Nye and her sister, Birdie Walker who was on line 16,
tended to visit over the phone quite a lot. I recall one instance
when Dad was trying to get a call through to a farmer about buying his cattle, and Minnie and Birdie were involved in one of
their extended conversations. After three of so raisings of the
receiver, Dad asked Minnie if he could use the phone briefly for a
call, to which Minnie apparently replied "no" and that she paid
the same amount of money as he did for phone service, to which
he replied "Yes, but I don't use the damn thing all the time."
Their relationship was always cool. Dad didn't buy many cattle
from Minnie.

As I look back, I realize that the Butler Telephone Company
and its party lines were an essential part of our lives; at the same
time, both helpful and irritating. The loss of privacy was balanced
by the instant links with the rest of the community. It is comforting to remember the general call warning us of the tornado that
struck the McFarland farm, the notice the Stanley players were
coming to town, and even listening in on the conversations
between Minnie and Birdie.

Like many other potential capitalistic entrepreneurs, I wish I
had bought up all of those lovely oak telephone boxes as they
have been replaced by digital telephones and all that privacy... or
is it isolation?

HALLOWEEN PRANKS

Halloween during my teen years seemed to convey the understanding that one had a temporary permit to be ornery, though not to be mean. No doubt it provided a night where no responsible adult felt truly comfortable, especially the parents of teenagers, or anyone who owned property.

There were no organized parties to keep youth off the streets, and there was little law enforcement to keep down the mischief. To my knowledge there was little "trick or treating" in those days, and if there was, we teenagers wouldn't have been caught dead doing it. In our circle, there were tricks but no treating.

There was a real attempt to be creative and funny. However, after the many years of Halloween nights, it was difficult for us to come up with something creative, or humorous. We did the usual mundane stuff, such as turning over privies (excusing those belonging to widows and older people). Almost everyone had a privy except bankers and doctors, and the challenge was to find a way to comment on these more affluent persons.

We resorted to placing barrels and other large objects in the streets, which provided selected opportunities to comment on privileged, though 'priviless', persons. Tricks such as hooking a long wire to the middle of a window screen, and then strumming the wire from a safe distance had promise, but never seemed to work out very well, especially on people who had inside dogs or outside lights.

One inspired Halloween night, we decided to tie one of Joe Gill's goats to the Butler fire bell, which was located at the base of the water tower, to see if the goat alone could ring the bell. The bell was a replica of the Liberty Bell, set on a concrete slab and rung by pulling on the rope tied to the top of the bell. The criteria for such a prank seemed well met. Joe was an irascible guy, and we were sure no lasting harm would come to the goat or to the fire bell.

On that night, my friends and I were riding around in our family car, a 1931 Ford Model A sedan. As did most cars in those days, it had outside running boards, and our plan was to stand a goat on one of the running boards and for one of us to hold it pinned to the car with our knees while we held on the center post between the rolled down windows. I recall, perhaps erroneously, that Jack Hill drove the car. I am certain I held the goat on the side of the car. We could hear Joe hollering as we took off to the water tower with his bleating goat.

We tied the hapless animal to the fire bell rope. The upshot of this Halloween episode was that the goat rang the bell frantically, and, for us, quite joyously. The down side for me was that we had selected a virile, old billy goat that stank horribly. It took a complete change of clothes, two baths and two days for me to rid myself of the foul odor, which was nauseating and very certainly linked me to the antic. My conscience has often thought it was just retribution for the embarrassment to the goat.

Some older culprits carried out a classic prank one year. They disassembled a full-sized farm wagon, raised it piece by piece to the roof of Ben Nye's furniture store and reassembled it on the crest of the roof. It remained there several days, with no one apparently wanting to encounter Ben's wrath by admitting to the act. Ben was a huge person who didn't smile a lot. He was also the local undertaker. Actually, it was an eye-catching addition to the store and, perhaps, an advertising display ahead of its time.

One of the pranks we pulled occasionally was to place a privy on the landing at the front entrance of the Butler Bank. There was usually a prominent sign that read, "Make your deposits here". On the next day, at our parents' insistence we would return the privy to its rightful place. It seemed that no one minded being associated with this comment on the haughty status of the bank and its owners, so long as we returned the privy to accommodate its owner.

Which suddenly reminds me! Who took the goat home?

Note from the author:

ERRATA: On pages 47 & 48, 'James <u>Henry</u> Beers'
            should read,   'James <u>Albert</u> Beers"
Ironically, this chapter is about the importance of middle names.
I make a sincere apology to James for this error which was
brought to my attention after the manuscript had gone to press.

James was one of the best athletes I have known and one
of the finest gentlemen.
James Albert, we'll make the correction to the text should this little
volume go to second printing.

                                                    - Roger Lee

MIDDLE NAMES

Most of us are given three names at birth, and more if outrageous relatives must be appeased. My three are Roger, Lee and Duncan. Somehow, not a lot of my new relatives felt strongly about my being named after them. I was told that 'Roger' came from my dad's admiration for Rogers Hornsby, a major league baseball player and manager. Dad dropped the 's', so he said, because farm people don't go too much for plural names.

'Lee' came from General Lee, the Confederate soldier admired by many for his wealth and white horse, if not for his military leadership. Dad's middle name was also 'Lee', taken, no doubt from the same general.

A lot of people seem to think it hokey to be called by all of one's names, or by the first two in more casual conversation. Out in farm country, especially in Southern and most Southwestern states, people appeared to think that if you were given a middle name, it should be used. "Waste not, want not" guides a lot of farm behavior.

I remember the McKowan family that lived just north of us on a farm later bought by Jack Wright. They had nine daughters, all quite pretty in comparison with other girls in the community. Their three oldest girls were called Anna Maude, Donna Leita and Mary Charlotte. I doubt I would have remembered their names for this long a time if they had been called simply Anna, Donna and Mary. Incidentally, the tenth McKowan child was a boy. I have forgotten his given name, but do recall that he was called 'Brother Son'.

When I was coaching athletics at Putnam, Oklahoma High School, I took one of our athletes, James Henry Beers, to Oklahoma Baptist University to try out for one of their varsity teams. Everyone there was most gracious. The coach, Bob Bass, asked us if we would like to meet James Lee, the University's president. I said that we would like very much to meet President Lee if it was convenient for him. Mr. Bass explained that the president's full name was Dr. James Lee Walker, but that out-of-town visitors often didn't know that.

Although Mr. Bass went on to become one of the top coaches

in the National Basketball Association, I have wondered what suc-
cesses he might have had if he had used all three of his names.
Incidentally, the University did award James Henry a scholarship
to play varsity baseball.

Even though French people seem to waste a lot of letters at
the ends of many of their words by not sounding them out, they
still often use middle names. How about Jean Claude Killey, the
noted skier, and Jean Luc Picard of Star Trek: The Next
Generation. Perhaps, if they didn't name so many of their boys
'Jean', even they wouldn't think middle names to be important.

It is often important for us to use all our given names for
sure identification. If I won the lottery I would be disappointed if
it was given to a Roger Claude Duncan, and if a process server
had a summons for a Roger Luc Duncan, I would like to be
spared an appearance in court.

When I was a youngster, my folks used my middle name
strictly for effect, not identification. I knew I was in for a heap of
trouble when I heard, "Roger Lee Duncan, you get yourself in
this house this minute". Movie stars, however, may use middle
names for both effect and for identification. One may not recognize the name 'Lou Phillips', but can identify Lou Diamond
Phillips for the fine actor he is - and then hasten to see his latest
flick.

I have decided it is neither fey nor overkill for us to use all
our given names. It isn't a lot of trouble, especially for me since
my middle name has only three letters, two of which are the
same.

A ONE HORSEPOWER HAY BALER

These days, when I see an air conditioned pickup baler rolling across a field, picking up neatly raked rows of loose hay and spitting out perfectly formed bales, I sometimes wonder if the operator might be lonesome.

Being lonesome at haying time during the 1930's was not a problem, at least not in western Oklahoma. Many of the farm tasks were labor intensive, but few more than putting up hay. There was much camaraderie and community involvement in the building of haystacks and, especially, baling the hay with a stationary baler.

During the 1930's and 40's, most farmers stored their hay by building ubiquitous haystacks. Theoretically, rain water sloped off the angled stacks, much like a thatched roof. Several problems accompanied these rather simple-seeming, natural procedures. Hay, or portions of it, often molded or rotted despite care in handling it. Another problem was the difficulty feeding it from the stack to livestock as they needed it. It was frustrating to try to lift pitchforks of hay while still standing on it - or when layers of hay seemed to overlap the one you were trying to remove from the stack. One approach to the problem of feeding stacked hay consisted of sawing it as one would a loaf of bread and then feeding the slices to the livestock.

The easy way out, at feeding time, was to take down the protective fence and let the stock, usually cattle and horses, simply eat through the stack as they wished. The stack took on a storybook appearance, looking like a giant mushroom as the cows and horses ate through it at eye level. This was expedient but somewhat wasteful. Farmers hated to see hay trampled into the ground, especially if it was their own good alfalfa.

Jack Wright, whose farm joined ours to the north, took great pains to see that his precious alfalfa hay was not wasted. He packaged it in neat rectangular bales and stored it his dry barn, all of which required considerable ingenuity and hard work. During the 1930's, the state of the art in hay baling was not extremely high. And it took a sizable amount of cooperation from friends and neighbors. Fortunately labor was a ready commodity in those days, which was fortunate for many of the tasks - especially baling hay. Many farm families, such as the Wright's and ours, "traded out" labor with one another. As a result, little money changed hands for labor costs. Bartering in those days was simple and often involved only time, one of the few fairly and widely distributed resources.

The hay baler was located at the edge of the alfalfa field. It was an interesting contraption, having two separate components connected by a round metal rod about 20 feet long and an inch and a half in diameter. The shaft was positioned about six inches off the ground, and it transmitted one horsepower of work, less a bit lost through friction, from one unit to the other.

The power unit consisted of a horse walking a circumference of a twenty foot diameter circle, pulling a lever attached to a central vertical axle. As the axle turned, a cam at the bottom of the axle converted its circular motion into a back-and-forth, pumping action of the long shaft. The horse was expected to step over the shaft as it completed its trek around its ever deepening path. Totally boring for a horse.

The other part of the machine baled the hay. Loose hay was placed in a hopper at one end of a long rectangular frame. A plunger moved back and forth in the frame and pressed the hay into bales, with the horse providing power for the plunger as it moved back and forth.

The hay had been cut down by a sickle mower drawn by two horses. It was raked into rows and then into piles with a horse drawn rake. The hay was finally brought to the bailer with a buck rake or by wagons. The loose hay was handled carefully to keep the leaves from falling from the stems. It was important for the hay to be cured properly, not too wet and green that it would become moldy in the bale, and not so dry that the leaves would shatter during the baling process.

At the hay baler, one person forked the loose hay onto a plat-form by the hopper. One person, the feeder, stuffed a quantity of hay down into the hopper, either with a pitchfork with sawed off tines or with his foot. Needless to say, feeding the baler with one's foot presented nightmarish risks, but was the more effi-cient way. I learned in later years from my older brother, that Dad once had the heel of his shoe ripped off as the plunger moved through the hopper. Apparently Dad was not injured, at least, not physically. I was too young to feed the baler, and I was quite pleased to leave it that way.

As the plunger came back to press the hopper-full of hay through the rectangular form, the horse strained momentarily. If the horse lagged, one person, usually a youngster, urged him on with a sharp word or a touch of a wooden switch. There was a back-up horse standing by to relieve the other when it was evi-dent the horse was tired. I often worried that the horse might become dizzy, but that never seemed to be a problem.

The length of the bales was set when the feeder placed a wooden block, instead of hay, into the hopper. These wooden blocks were shaped to fit the frame that formed the bales. Each wooden block had four horizontal grooves, two on either side through which wires were pushed to tie the bales. One person, the tyer, started the looped ends of two wires through the blocks and another person, the threader, pushed them back through at the other end of the bale. The tyer then attached the ends of the wire to one another, and the threader stacked the new bales as they dropped from the end of the baler. He also toted the wood-en block back up to the feeder.

The tyer had the responsibility of telling the feeder when to drop in a wooden block. He would shout either, "Block her down" or "Down and block" and thus set the length of the bale. There was little sound except for human voices and the occasion-al snorting of one of the horses. Talk was either concerned with the hay baling tasks or with idle, often humorous, chatter. We youngsters came in for a share of teasing, particularly when a lack of experience or strength came to bear on our tasks.

When the day was done, we all loaded the bales onto the wagons and stacked them safely in the barn. It was a relief to clean the dirt and sweat from our bodies and to remove the itchy, scratchy alfalfa leaves from under our shirt collars. This was no easy task, what with the absence of shower baths in most farm homes. I recall the good feeling of being tired, but buoyed by the thoughts of a good day's work.

One day the sequence of baling events was interrupted when the shaft broke into two pieces. Jack asked me if I wanted to help him take the shaft to town to have it fixed. I was excited and quite proud to be asked. Not only would I find out how to fix a break such as this, but I would have some time to spend with Jack. He was not only a great person, but he also had played semi-pro baseball in Clovis, New Mexico and starred on the Butler town team. All of the other members of the crew went home while Jack and I hitched a team of horses to a wagon and trotted them off to town.

We took the broken shaft into G. Small's blacksmith shop in Butler where Mr. Small was to join the two pieces. I was fascinated by his magical and brawny efforts. He heated the two broken ends until they were cherry red, placed them on his huge anvil and beat the end into a long tapered wedge with a substantial hammer. He then overlapped the reheated ends at the exact place and hammered them until they were melded. With his hammer, he shaped the shaft until it appeared to be perfectly round. It was difficult to find where the break had occurred, and I wondered at his artistry.

We then loaded the shaft, surprisingly long as one piece, onto the wagon; and it was back to Jack's alfalfa patch, where the horse began once again its circular trek, the plunger went back and forth and the tyer sang out, "Down and block".

INSURANCE, DEPRESSION STYLE

One of the things I have learned in my adult years is the importance of insurance. It is an expensive and, in many instances, a required commodity. However, during my youth I wasn't aware that people thought much about insurance. I don't recall a serious discussion by anyone concerning the need for it.

There was a basic trust of others and an overriding sense that one simply did the right thing. There was pride in the knowledge that one's word was one's bond, and many significant deals were sealed with a handshake. People felt responsibility for their actions and made amends in cash, goods or services as best they could. I am certain that few people thought they might pay in advance to assure they would not suffer from acts of nature, others' actions or from their own errors.

An illustration of this general attitude is a story about Herman 'Big' Phillips. One day during the 1930s, 'Big', who lived southwest of Butler on a farm in the Washita Valley, was driving his pickup down the road toward town when his truck was sideswiped by a neighbor woman. Her name may have been Edith Metcalf.

Country roads in the Butler area were narrow and neither paved nor graveled. The farm roads were not well maintained and were often rutted and rough. Meeting another automobile coming down one of them could be a nervous experience. According to Herman, Edith said that the collision was her fault and she felt really bad about it. Herman said he told her, to the contrary, it was his fault because he saw her coming a full quarter of a mile away and that he could have easily pulled into a wheat field alongside the road while she passed by. Everyone laughed at his version of the incident, and Edith paid to have his pickup repaired.

When I was nineteen years old, and a sophomore in college at Weatherford, Oklahoma, I was involved in what could easily have been a fatal automobile collision, I was driving our farm pickup down Highway 66 between Clinton and Weatherford, going back to the college for a flight test. My two younger brothers and a neighbor boy were with me in the cab of the pickup.

This particular strip of Highway 66, like most of the famous coast-to-coast highway, was an often curving, narrow two-lane road, quite difficult to navigate, especially in an old farm pickup with questionable steering and brakes. The roadbed was paved with concrete and had a raised lip on each edge of the road, presumably to prevent erosion of the shoulders, but realistically, made driving even more hazardous.

Driving too fast, I had to attempt to go around a slow-moving car to avoid rear ending it. To my horror, I saw a another car approaching from the opposite direction. Our bumpers overlapped about twelve inches, and I watched, sick, as the other car slid, screeching on one of its sides, down the concrete pavement. The other car contained the driver, his wife and a young child. It was, indeed, a miracle that no one was injured.

After we had been given a ride into Weatherford, I called Dad to tell him about the collision. He said for us to hold tight, that he would be coming through Weatherford on the following day taking a load of cattle to the market in Oklahoma City, and that he would talk to the driver of the other car.

After the driver's well-justified first burst of anger, he turned out to be a pretty decent fellow. He said that he was an oil field worker going back home to Bakersfield, California. Their car was a 1932 Essex Terraplane. He said that he'd given $75 for it and stilled owed $50 in payments. He told Dad that he would settle for $100 to pay for train tickets home, and that the mortgage company could come for the car if they wanted it. I watched nervously as Dad talked him down to $70. For years after the accident I carried in my wallet the signed agreement absolving us of any future claims related to the collision. I carried the sense of guilt much longer.

We had the pickup repaired at a Weatherford garage for $125 and I was assessed an $18 fine for careless driving. The total costs, seeming small today, were difficult for my family to cover. I gratefully worked on the farm instead of going to college during the next semester.

J.R. Bibb, a good friend who grew up on a farm near ours, has a thought-provoking view about automobile 'accidents'. 'Big' Phillips' collision and mine give credence to J.R.'s contention that there are no automobile 'accidents'. His attitude is that automobile collisions are caused by someone's error, poor judgment or, in rare cases, by intent. To him, they should not be excused as acts of chance.

Obtaining health care was a concern during the depression days, much as it is now. People back then, however, didn't consider paying for medical attention until it was received. I doubt that anyone was denied doctors' services because they couldn't pay for it.

There were two excellent doctors in Butler, Dr. Bassinger and Dr. Hinshaw. Both made house calls and referred patients to one another when they were out of town or were otherwise indisposed, and Dr. Hinshaw's office operated from a small hospital he owned.

The charges for doctors' services seemed quite reasonable. Many of the costs were reduced or forgiven if the patient's family was having a hard time with finances. Most babies were born at home, with family or neighbors helping to care for the young babes and mothers during and after the birth.

People in the community were tuned in to those who might be in need of help because of illnesses. A neighbor of ours was stricken with a lengthy illness, and other neighbors and we laid his cotton by in one short day. I felt very good and personally secure at being part of this contribution to his family. It was fascinating to see six or more horse drawn cultivators and 20 or so cotton choppers sweep across his cotton field. The <u>Butler Herald</u> would at times report that someone needed nursing help or that a fund had been set up for much needed assistance. Often a hat would be passed at a baseball game or at churches to help someone pay medical bills.

The ratio of doctors to lawyers in Butler was two to none. Perhaps life was simple enough that no one needed any legal complications explained to them or were too busy with the chores of living to make a big thing of injustices.

One insurance plan many farmers chose when they took on a

mortgage to purchase a farm included a mortgage cancellation clause that provided the mortgage would be forgiven if the husband died. This seemed like a reasonable thing to do in that it assured a man's family could continue to have a place to stay and a way to survive by operating or selling the farm.

These days, we may sometimes hear the expression 'he bought the farm' to indicate someone's death, whether or not that person was a farmer. However, when the phrase originated, the death of a farmer with mortgage insurance really did mean, "he bought the farm".

A COTTON PICKING VACATION

There is little doubt that the demands of farm life strongly influenced the school calendar when I was in grade and high school in western Oklahoma. This still may be the case in much of rural America. Although this tradition is oft-times impugned by industrialists, educators, parents and students alike, it was and is a natural and important part of farm and family life.

Not only did schools let out during the summer growing season, but during the harvests as well. This was particularly true about cotton farming. There was a window between the time the cotton bolls opened and the cotton fell out on the ground that required an immense amount of human effort and oft-times onerous labor. With the development of strains of cotton that are resistant to various wastes and the development of sophisticated mechanical harvesters, advances in technology have made such massive turnouts of people for cotton harvest today unnecessary.

The main part of cotton harvest happened in the Fall when school work would just be getting into full swing. According to the wisdom of rural school boards, the prudent thing to do was to start school early in the year when the crops had been laid by and then to dismiss school so that students could help harvest the cotton. This respite from school was called "cotton-picking vacation"- and other names, I am sure. Presently, this term would qualify, for sure, as an oxymoron.

"Cotton-picking" took on a mildly derisive meaning in some of the rural vernacular through expressions like "the cotton-picking car won't start" or "the cotton-picking wind blew dirt in the milk".

Picking cotton, generally, was not a lot of fun. It required pulling a long sack, bending to pull the bolls of cotton from the stalks or the locks of cotton from the ground and putting them in the sack. Crawling on knees provided rest for the back, with resulting costs to the knees. Back said "Get down" and knees said, "Get back up". Hands always paid a price.

Incidentally, "picking" cotton for our time was a misnomer. "Snapping" or "pulling" cotton would have been more nearly correct. Originally, the cotton 'locks' (fiber and seeds) were picked from the hulls of the bolls on the stalks; however, the further development of cotton gins enabled the locks to be separated from the hulls mechanically at the gin. In this "cotton-picking" business, all help was appreciated.

The only equipment one really needed for picking cotton was a cotton sack. Gloves were often used, and you could tell who were the 'pros' by their knee pads.

There were no designer sacks or gloves. Whenever possible, last year's sacks were used. Old sacks with holes were often patched. The shoulder strap could be resewn so that the less worn side of the sack was on the bottom. Straps were padded if need be to help prevent chafing. And if there were good cotton gloves for the right hand but not for the left, a left-handed glove was created by turning one of the gloves inside-out.

Cotton sacks varied in length according to certain factors. The major factors were the drive, and the physical and ego strength of individual workers. A very strong person would usually pull a sack 16 to 20 feet long if he really wished to earn his Max for the day. It simply enabled him to spend more time picking and less time toting the filled sack to the scales, weighing and emptying it. Needless to say, a considerable amount of energy was expended in these tasks. The rear end of the longer sacks were left unsewn and were tied with a heavy cord or leather strap which could be removed to make emptying the sack easier.

Younger persons or those with less strength ordinarily would pull sacks six to ten feet long. The rear end of these sacks were usually sewn shut and the cotton was emptied after it was weighed by elevating the rear end of the bag and giving it a quick shake.

For obvious reasons, the scales were placed as close as possible to the geographic center of the area of the cotton patch currently being harvested. The scales inevitably were of a balance design with a metal weight or "pea" that was moved down the scale until the scale beam was level. Generally, the scales were suspended six feet or so above the ground in one of three ways: from a board extended from the back of a truck, from the tongue of a wagon propped up by the wagon's yoke or simply from a tripod of long, stout poles.

The symbol of the wagon with its uplifted tongue has stayed with me, perhaps because it seemed to represent a more natural way to complete a segment of farm life. With wagons, there were no intrusions of noisy, smelly truck engines or wastes of cotton by piling it on the ground beside the tripods.

The weighing of the cotton presented the most gracious and restful times for the day. The approach of one person to the scales often prompted others to join in, whether or not their sacks were filled to capacity. There was usually light chatter, often with commiseration with one another. Backs were rested, thirsts were quenched and face-to-face contacts were made.

There was a surprising intimacy in looking at another's face when your consuming view for sometime had been cotton stalks and the occasional picture of a cotton sack alongside or the backside of a fellow worker. I often saw freckles or lines on familiar faces that I had not noted before.

Probably the most important part, however, was the spirit of being together in an ordinarily solitary venture and of helping one another. The strong helped the strong and the less strong, lifting the sacks up to be attached to the scales for weighing, hefting the sacks into the wagon, truck or pile and then emptying the often tightly packed sacks. Other folk supported their fellows with libations, comforts, needed repairs, care for the young and pats on the back.

There was also the business of the work day to be undertaken. The farmer was often there at the weighing site to help weigh, to keep track of the weights of the cotton and, often, to observe the condition of the cotton as it came from the sacks.

Obviously, since workers were paid by the pounds of cotton they gathered, there was a need for one to work as fast as one could. This tended to cause the workers to be a bit cavalier as to what went into their sacks. For example, long stems often came off with the bolls, and care would say that they should be broken off and not placed in the sack; green leaves, if the picking was before frost had come, often went into the sack; the same applied to green unopened bolls, which had not dried and were quite weighty; and there was always the problem of picking up dirt with the locks of cotton that had dropped from the burrs onto the ground.

These added bits of waste all affected the grade of the cotton after it was ginned and the price the farmer was paid for the finished bale. These bits added to the weight of the cotton in the pickers' sacks, which also cost the farmer. Quite naturally, this all added to the excitement of emptying one's sack in view of the farmer, or of fastidious pickers. I have heard pickers being chided over the color of their gatherings, including my own, but I don't recall anyone's having been fired over it. For some, the adage was, "I put in the sack only what comes off in my hands, and that all belongs to the farmer".

One did not make high wages picking cotton. When the conditions for picking were at their very best - lots of open bolls and no green leaves - some very strong, dedicated men might pick a thousand pounds in a long day, but they were few, and far between. I personally was never able to pick more than 600 pounds in one day.

In our family, my younger brother Joe was the best picker. He made it look easy. He never hurried with his labor; his hands seemed to wander magically among the cotton plants as he filled his sack more quickly than the rest of us. I always had the feeling that he never looked at what was in his hands and simply stuffed it in his sack.

Hudie Ledbetter, better known as 'Leadbelly', wrote and sang several songs about picking cotton. One went something like:

Jump down, turn around, pick a bale of cotton;
Jump down, turn around, pick a bale a day.
Me and my wife can pick a bale of cotton;
Me and my wife can pick a bale a day.

I thought, "Man, that's a lot of cotton". But I never doubted they could do it. Incidentally, it took about 1800 pounds of raw cotton in those days to yield a finished bale of fiber weighing 500 pounds, which seemed to be the standard weight.

Many women picked cotton, often alongside other members of their families. It was not unusual to see women pulling a sack with an infant riding on it. The need to earn money or simply to complete the harvest was widespread. For many, one of the few money crops was raising or picking cotton.

Although one might not think of western Oklahoma as an important cotton growing area, cotton produced considerable action and revenue; enough,in fact, to attract migrant workers. Families from eastern Oklahoma and from Arkansas came west during the height of the cotton harvest. Usually, each family would arrive in a truck, which served dual purposes. Not only would the truck provide transportation for the family, it also was a tool of the harvest. The family would agree with a farmer to pick cotton, load it into their truck and take it to the gin, all for a prearranged financial package. The gin operators, in harmony with both, would pay the wages and hauling costs to the working family and the balance to the farmer.

One of the added joys of having these migrant workers in our community was their very presence. They were honest, hard-working people, qualities that wore well. Although they tended to be shy and retiring, there was considerable interaction with the local residents. We didn't travel around much, at least not in our family, and my contact with these visitors was fascinating to me, even though most of them were from my home state.

Our major differences seemed to me to be in our speech patterns. For example, some of them tended to 'regularize' their verbs, to say 'seed' where we said 'saw'; to say 'heared' where we would say 'heard' and 'knowed' instead of 'knew'. An expression they might use would be,"I heared that John was interested, and I knowed it was so because I seed him talking to the banker." I recall wondering if they lived in a region that had remained isolated from the rest of the world, retaining olden speech patterns such as those brought here by English settlers.

On several occasions during the cotton picking vacations, I would go with Dad to take a load of cotton in to town to be ginned. These were fun happenings. There were two busy gins in Butler, the Farmers' Gin and Cox's Gin. We usually went to Farmer's, perhaps because it may have been part of a co-op to which we belonged. It was fun to go to either, but more interesting to go to Cox's.

Mr. Cox provided power for his gin with a steam engine, which was located out in the open air beside the main building. I was fascinated as I watched a long rod move back and forth causing a large wheel to spin. I could see the valves open and close and hear the steam escape. I had never seen power created and transferred in such a way.

When it was time for our load to be ginned, the truck or wagon would be moved under a long suction tube about a foot in diameter. The suction operator would move the lower end of the tube around over the top of the load of cotton until all of it had been vacuumed into the ginning machinery. Sometimes the operator would show off for the youngsters by taking off his hat and holding the tube over his head. His hair would stand straight on end, much to our surprise and delight.

We could then view the finished bale of cotton fiber, strangely small now, covered by a loosely woven brown net and bound tightly by narrow black steel bands. The buyer would cut out a small bit to look at the fibers, and to judge its quality based on fiber length, color and whether there were contaminants such as dirt and fragments of stems, leaves and green cotton bolls. The evaluations contained terms such as 'fair' and 'middling'. At that moment, it was hard to relate it all to the rather cavalier way we had stuffed the cotton in our sacks back in the field.

The cotton seed, now cleanly separated from the locks of fiber, was sold also, later to be processed into cottonseed meal for use as livestock feed. I am sure that many other uses of this by-product of cotton picking are made today. Dad said that the seed "paid for the ginning".

The burrs and other trash were blown through an elevated pipe at the rear of the ginning building to form an ever-growing mountain of rough, brown shredded plant material, all to be burned when the wind was blowing from the right direction during the winter months.

As we returned to the farm, thoughts of the softness of the finished cotton fiber, the feel of the solid cotton seeds in the cotton locks, the rough points and edges of burrs that had torn at the skin of our hands, flitted through my mind. In retrospect, as we returned, virtually empty-handed, we might well have thought of the loss to the land which was, in the end, the great loser. We had used the land, much of which should never have been put to the plow, especially the up-land, to sustain our family in a very costly, though immediately significant, effort.

The time we spent out of the classroom for cotton harvest usually lasted from four to six weeks. I was always glad for this 'vacation' to be over, even though it meant going back to hit the cotton-picking books.

DOC' BIBB

J. R. Bibb and I both attended our two room neighborhood school called New Home for eight years, and later Butler High school. He was one grade behind me all the way, and I think he was a couple of years younger than I. He and his older brother, H.B., took the West road from New Home School, and my siblings and I took the South road. The Bibbs lived about two and a half miles from New Home and usually rode horses to school. As did we.

J. R. and I spent considerable time together both at school and on weekends. It was fun to go to his place. It was a combination of a farm and ranch, it seemed to me.

J.R.'s grandfather lived on a real live ranch about two miles from their place. His grandfather had a license to pack a gun, being a deputy sheriff on call or something like that. He wore a huge pistol under the unbuttoned side of his overalls when he came to Butler, reminding me that we were not too far in time from the Old West. I have a feeling that his grandfather had a considerable influence on J.R. Both had a no nonsense attitude toward the business of life and retained an unquestioned loyalty to their friends.

When I visited J. R., I always expected and enjoyed an exciting time. We did the usual farm chores, milking several cows, in this case white-faced range cattle. J. R. said they didn't give a lot of milk, but what they produced was of high quality. I recall the wonderful, strong coffee his mom, Katie, made and served in huge mugs with rich cream.

I remember, vividly, hunting squirrels and rabbits with J.R. and H.B., made more memorable because we didn't have any guns at our house. I was impressed at the Bibb boys' marksmanship and their knowledge of guns. On one squirrel-hunting excursion with H.B., he asked me to climb a tree and scare out any squirrel that might be lying in a squirrel nest high in one of the trees growing along the creek that ran through their place. I did so, and a squirrel scrambled from the nest, I heard H.B. shout, "Duck", which I quickly did, and a loud bang. I escaped unscathed, but not the hapless squirrel.

During our high school years, J.R. and I hung out together quite a bit, often with Paul Starks and Jack Hill, going to Hammon for the late hour preview of movies on Saturday nights, stealing watermelons and doing Halloween pranks. Incidentally, I am not sure but that J.R. was the driver of the car when we tied Joe Gill's goat to the fire bell one Halloween night.

We actually did school work and, also, played on the high school basketball team. One of my prized photographs is of our team along with one of our debatable heroes, Coach Champ Davis. J.R. is the handsome, smiling young player Number 44, kneeling in the front row.

After high school, our paths separated for a while. Following a stint in the Army, J.R. became a chiropractor in Dallas, successful in his practice and being part of Dallas as it grew from a cow town to the sophisticated metropolis of today. I went into the Navy, became a schoolteacher and finally settled near Denver. J.R. comes to Colorado now and then, and we enjoy his visits, with life becoming a bit different and more interesting while he is here and most enjoyable.

Following my retirement, I continued to live in Golden, near Denver, with my family. One day the telephone rang, and I heard J.R.'s unmistakable voice. He asked what kind of a car I was driving, and I replied that I was driving a Fairmont station wagon, which I thought, incidentally, he had seen on one of his earlier trips to Denver.

He explained that he was retiring from his practice, and part of his retirement plans was to get rid of an extra car he had, and he wanted to give it to me. He explained further that I knew he took good care of his cars (He had been a mechanic in the Army). He said it was a Brougham, a name that meant nothing to me. Quite selfishly, I said, "Sure". He also said it needed new front tires. I located my Sears card to front the cost of tires.

We set a date for me to pick up the car, with a planned couple of days for me to get the car ready for the trip home. I took a Greyhound bus to Dallas, an overnighter that stopped in every small town on the way through southern Colorado, New Mexico and Texas. I thoroughly enjoyed the trip. The plains are my kind of country, and I farmed, in my mind, every piece of land on the way.

J.R. is a well organized person, and I explained the details of the trip to him before I left Denver. He seemed to be a bit surprised that I was to arrive at the bus station rather than the Dallas/Fort Worth airport.

The bus was on time, as was J.R. He led me casually to my new car parked on the street close to the bus station. It was an immaculate Wax Berry Yellow Cadillac. Speechless, I finally said the front tires seemed OK, and he explained that he had had to drive the car to Arkansas, and he put on new tires before the trip. We got into the car to drive to his house. This was the first time I had ridden in a car with finished split-leather seats.

My stay in Dallas was good for me. I learned a lot about J.R. and about mutual friends and our relatives. You can be sure that I learned a lot about the care of one Cadillac Brougham automobile. More importantly, I became reacquainted with an old friend, reliving much of our rich childhood together and understanding that, like his grandfather, he knew how to take care of business and to be responsive to his friends. My definition of friendship broadened considerably.

When I drove away North in my elegant car with its new front tires and my Sears credit card pressed cool in my billfold against the soft leather seat, I suddenly remembered that he is known as Dr. J.R. Bibb in Dallas, and that only one person, other than I, knew his full name is James Radford Bibb.

CHRISTMAS BY CANDLELIGHT

There was a time when I looked forward to Christmas with great joy. Christmas at our house when I was a youngster during the late twenties and thirties was special, though not associated with extravagant gifts or elaborate decorations. There was a feeling of anticipation as it approached, a joy of celebration and a sense of fulfillment as it came to an end.

The preparation for Christmas was orchestrated by Mom. What a strong, effective woman this slight, quiet person could be. Cakes and pies were baked well in advance to be ready for the main meal, which was served about noontime on Christmas Day. The meat dish had been selected. If it was fowl, the creature met its fate early Christmas morning, since we had no way to refrigerate the meat.

We all pitched in, with divisions of labor assigned according to strengths, not interests and desires. I dreaded beheading, scalding and plucking the birds. The odor of wet hot feathers lingers still in my mind. I really would have chosen to work with Mom in the kitchen.

Selecting, making or buying gifts were not as overpowering then as it seems to be today. If a gift was purchased, it was usually ordered from the Sears Roebuck or Montgomery Ward catalogues. There was little advertising in the media to spur the wanting of particular items. Gift giving was not a big thing. Children received one major gift bought by Mom and Dad in Santa's name. It would be found in the living room on Christmas morning. Usually toys were received when we were young; clothes when we were older. I recall, fondly, helping Mom wrap wind-up, crawling tractors for my younger brothers. Before wrapping them, we both enjoyed seeing how many books we needed to stack to make the tractors fall over backwards as they attempted to climb them. Needless to say, neither Mom nor I got to touch them again.

Recently, I surveyed my siblings about gift giving at Christmas time. None of us recalls giving gifts to one another when we were younger. Our parents didn't fare very well, either. We did not put up and trim a Christmas tree at home. Evergreen trees did not thrive in our part of the country and decorating a bare branch as a Christmas tree, which my English wife does on occasion, never crossed our minds.

However, we did get to enjoy the presence of a Christmas tree. Each Christmas Eve, the New Home community held a Christmas party at the local school, an event important to all of us. Some of the men of the community would take one of their trucks and bring a Cedar tree back from the South Canadian River, which ran about 20 miles to the north of our farm. It was always an impressive tree that occupied much of the stage in the two-room school building. The tree was then decorated with strings of popcorn and cranberries, shining streams of tinsel and colorful baubles. As people came into the building, they "oohed and awed" at its magnificence.

The tree was not lighted. There was no rural electrification in our part of the country at that time. Our parents apparently thought there were enough hazards already in a crowded wooden building heated by wood stoves and lighted with gasoline and kerosene lamps. Incidentally, The Country Gentlemen have recorded a tragic song about the effects of a school fire in a similar setting that haunts me still, and causes me to appreciate the wisdom of our parents. Our Christmas tree did not need lights to be beautiful, or to be appreciated.

The students in the school put on most of the evening's program. The teachers insisted that all students participate in the program, and we all bravely cooperated. Even the shyest went on stage if just to deliver a four line poem, sometimes inaudible with half of it presented on the way to the center of the tree-crowded stage and the other half during the dash off the stage. There was no opposition to the Christmas program on religious or sectarian grounds. There were several songs and plays and poems about the birth of Jesus. We all knew why we were celebrating the occasion.

After the program, Santa Claus would burst through the door with, the customary 'Merry Christmas' and a flood of 'Ho, ho, ho's. Usually Walt Fox was Santa, and he relished the task. Although memory may be too kind to Walt here, I thought him to be quite good, and - for the young - believable. I judge he could have been a big hit at Macy's. Some parents, but not all, brought gifts to the event for their children, and there were gifts to and from the two teachers. All gifts were handed to Walt, who either loudly called out the name on the gift, or let children crowded around him call out the names and then deliver them to the recipient.

Then followed one of the good and rightful parts of the evening's activities, the passing out of individually packed bags of fruit, nuts and candy for everyone in attendance. The filled bags were called 'treats'. The parents in the community had donated money and time to buy and package large quantities of goodies. I am sure that some of the merchants in town also donated supplies or, at least, sold them at no profit to themselves.

Santa was in charge of passing out the treats, and he did it by family groups. For example, he would say, "Bibb, four", "Duncan, seven", and then later would hoot, especially if being played by Walt, "Triplet, three". After he had gone through the family list, he would say with full sincerity and invitation, "Is there anyone here who has not received a treat?" If a guest or a stranger was there, either he or she, or someone near them would raise a hand. I always have thought this may have been a major part, if not the only part, of someone's Christmas, particularly during hard times.

Back at home, we went to bed with a feeling of high expectation of the celebration next day. I am not certain when it began to dawn on me that Santa was a role that someone assumed - that the Santa on Christmas Eve at the schoolhouse was Walt and the Santa that placed the gifts in the living room and filled the stockings during the night was Mom and Dad. I would be disappointed to learn that this awareness came at a late stage, what with our not having a fireplace and the stove pipe being about five inches in diameter.

Dad ordinarily was the first to arise in the morning, to build a fire in the wood stove and then to call out, "Fire's hot". On Christmas morning the routine was the same. I could hear him stirring around, with me wondering, momentarily, if it was Santa or my dad, even when he opened the stove door. I waited anxiously for 'fire's hot' and the mad scramble to the stove, pants and other clothes in hand. As we all gathered around the stove, all in a like state of undress, Norman Rockwell would have had a model for a painting that have would brought mixed emotions from all of us and nostalgia to last forever.

First, we opened our presents, tried out the toys, tried on the clothes or viewed other meaningful gifts (Our oldest brother, Tom, recalls with great satisfaction, receiving Hurlbert's Stories of the Bible). Then we went about exploring and consuming the contents of our stockings. Consistently over many Christmases, the orange filled the toe, followed by an apple, a wide variety of nuts and a delicious assortment of candies. Many of the candies were not individually wrapped and stuck together in a multi- textured, multi-colored, soon-to-be sticky, delicious mess. I am not certain, in this series of events, when we put on our clothes. We did know that soon we would hear Mom's admonition to stop eating candy and to "leave some room for dinner".

Dinner was not a spiritual happening; it was a sumptuous, rather pagan event. Mom was a superb country cook, and we five sturdy, growing children and Dad demonstrated our sincere appreciation. At times, we would have company to share our table, but most often it was a family celebration.

In the aftermath, we made good use of the remains of dinner. If we had turkey as the main dish, we carefully stripped the meat from the bones and ground it in a hand-cranked meat chopper for sandwiches. One of the downsides of eating at someone else's house, of course, was that one didn't have a turkey carcass to strip. Other leftovers provided Mom brief respite from cooking supper. They did not have chance to spoil at our house.

My memories of Christmas take on an added meaning as I view the ways many of us celebrate it today. Unfortunately, much of our attention is given to giving and receiving gifts. We seem to believe that we show love for someone by the value of our gift to them. And for the young, it takes on heightened excitement and stress as they have their wants and expectations incited by the compelling medium of television.

As a celebration, I will take Thanksgiving over Christmas these days, hands down. One of the best things about celebrating Christmas, for me, is recalling the ones gone by. How about cracking those nuts on the living room floor with a brick and hammer, and wincing as we stepped on the nut shells with our bare feet in the morning immediately after hearing 'fire's hot'? Ah, that's the kind of memory that stays with you, long after the wrappings have been thrown away.

GUINEAS AND ALBATROSSES

When I was a youngster, I wondered how birds flew. Not only the wild birds, but our domesticated ones, especially the guinea birds. They appeared to be only semi-domesticated, staying together as a flock, ranging far from the house, but coming back to the farmyard on occasion. They could fly for a full quarter mile. I don't know where they roosted, but they came home daily.

The guineas have a unique cry, "Petrack, petrack", and they are quite noisy when they are disturbed. Many farmers felt they provided an alarm system as they announced any intrusion into their assumed space. I was fascinated by the way the guineas landed in the farmyard, slowing as they approached the ground and cupping down their wings just before their feet touched the ground ever so lightly. I never saw one of them tumble as it landed.

I dreamed I could fly, holding my arms out and propelling myself the way Superman is depicted. The power came from within me, and I was able to fly over towns and fields, much to the wonderment of the people below on the ground. I don't remember dreams about landing; falling out of bed and hitting the floor probably would have awakened me.

I never dreamed I would ever be able to fly an airplane, until I went off to school at Southwestern State College in Weatherford, Oklahoma. I was surprised to learn the college offered a course in pilot training. The program was supported through a federal act, designed to bolster a fledgling aviation industry during the depression years. Its title was Civilian Pilot Training, or CPT. To my parents' horror, I enrolled in the aviation course. The price was right; the costs were included in my total college enrollment fee of $11 for the semester, and I would receive five semester credit hours in science upon successful completion of the training. Only in my later years did I know what a great deal this was. Later, the costs for learning to fly soon became prohibitive, especially for a person with the financial means of a family such as ours.

We trained in Piper Cub planes at an airport two or three

miles east of Weatherford. It was in the fall semester, 1941. The Japanese military forces attacked Pearl Harbor December 7, with the most devastating air and sea strikes ever launched. Its emotional impact on me was profound, and it may have given impetus to my wanting to fly well. It also gave me some negotiating room with my parents in the following years.

In 1941, there were no tricycle landing gears on airplanes that I had ever seen. All were "tail draggers". Landing a plane was tricky; one either made a full stall (three point) landing or, in strong or gusty winds, a much faster, front wheel landing which called for a soft touch down with a very slow rate of descent. A misjudgment in either type of landing usually resulted in a bouncing of the plane off the ground, much to the student pilot's embarrassment; and for a three point initial landing, a potentially dangerous situation.

Severe crosswinds often called for a one-wheel landing or takeoff. The development of tricycle landing gears eased many of the problems of landings and take offs with the center of gravity now being in front of the main wheels, although the techniques of Guinea birds in flight still applied.

I was saturated with admonitions that the most frequent cause of flying accidents was in the stalling of the plane. The plane simply must retain a certain speed to obtain adequate lift from its wings. If the required speed is not maintained the pilot loses control of the plane and gravity takes over. The most critical time for stalls is when a plane is taking off or climbing. A loss of speed through a nose high attitude or a loss of power can be devastating when the plane is near the ground.

In our training, we practiced not only recovery from stalls, but also from resulting spins, often planned and forced in our exercises and at safe altitudes. The spins seemed unnecessary, even then, as training practices, but they were fun. They were to be precision spins, usually for exactly two revolutions.

To enter a spin, the pilot lined up the plane with a visible road below. The nose of the plane was raised until the plane shuddered and stalled. The pilot would then kick one of the rudders into a full down position, watching the earth as the plane spiraled nose down. To recover from the spin, the stick was moved forward, the opposite rudder kicked at the correct moment for the plane to retain its course down the path above the road. It was a fairly vicious exercise. The pressure to learn such a maneuver came mainly from having to demonstrate this skill to a Civil Aeronautics Agency (CAA) examiner, who would give a test ride before certifying a private pilot's license.

The winds were with me on the day I took the flight test, and I was issued Pilot License Number 129710, a number which is mine forever. I also swore that I never wanted to be a CAA flight test examiner. Talk about placing your life in another's hands, and white knuckle flights! Pilot training has been stream-lined since World War 11 and made more appropriate for safe fly-ing practices. Modern pilot training is directed toward pilots' averting stall situations through skills learned through experienc-ing planned stalls and executing corrective maneuvers at safe alti-tudes. One does not spin the plane in modern practice; one averts spins.

For financial reasons I dropped out of school and worked for a while on the farm, exacting from Dad a promise that I could fly in the military when it was time. I was 19 years old. Older per-sons (including my brother Tom) had been drafted, and my time in military service was inevitable.

There was an Army Air Corps training base at El Reno, Oklahoma. Pilots trained there to fly Douglas A-20 attack bombers, a twin engine plane designed to operate with great speed and close to the ground. I could watch some of their prac-tice flights while I was working the corn field. I sensed the wind change and the leaves rustle from their low flights as they swept across the corn and then rose to disappear over the surrounding hills.

I decided to become an Army Air Corps pilot. With the draft near for me, I convinced my parents to let me join the Army avia-tion branch. I traveled by bus from Clinton to Oklahoma City to sign up. To my frustration, I found the line for applications for the Army Air Corps to be quite long. The recruiting line for Naval Aviation was much shorter, so I joined it, and the Navy. So much for commitment; but I, for sure, did not want to be drafted into the Army.

At the recommendation of one of my Navy flight instructors, I followed in his tradition and chose to fly sea planes. Later I wished he had selected the more acrobatic fighter planes, dive bombers or even torpedo planes based on aircraft carriers for our military service. I flew huge, lumbering twin-engine seaplanes on endless radar coverage of ship convoys and on rescue flights.

I was assigned to Patrol Bombing Squadron 210, operating from the Naval Air Station at Guantanamo, Cuba. We flew Martin Mariners (PBMs), reportedly the largest twin-engine seaplane in the world, and the least adequately powered.

Even in those relatively early days of aviation warfare, we carried "smart" bombs, much as today but which operated in a different medium, the ocean. In the engine nacelles of the PBMs we carried two highly secret sonic torpedoes that were designed to be attracted by engine noises made by enemy submarines; unfortunately, they were not smart enough to differentiate between enemy and friendly vessels. We were admonished not to drop them near the convoys. We carried more traditional depth bombs in the engine nacelles for close-in encounters.

Somehow, I never learned to trust the ocean, in part because of my lack of involvement with it as I grew up on a very dryland farm in Oklahoma. The ocean had absolutely no tradition for me to observe, and with its rolling swells did not provide an inviting place to land an airplane.

Ironically, upon my discharge from the Navy, I received from the CAA (later known as the FAA) a commercial certificate to fly multi-engine seaplanes, which I seldom had an opportunity to use out in western Oklahoma.

The Naval service was satisfying for me, and I thought my being a part of it to be important. Also, if I had a bed to sleep in, it was at least a dry one. But I longed to go back to the farm, to watch birds fly much better than I, even the guinea birds.

SELECTING A CAREER

After my discharge from the Navy, I enrolled once again at Southwestern State College at Weatherford, Oklahoma. My entry this time was quite different from six years before, when Mom had dragged me, a reluctant teenager, into the college president's office insisting that I be enrolled and have a job and a place to stay. He had complied; calling the local druggist who gave me a room above the store in exchange for cleaning the store seven mornings a week. Food came from our farm cellar and a few carefully saved dollars Mom would somehow scrounge from the cream and egg money.

This second time around I was a "Vet" with tuition and books and $75 a month provided by the GI Bill. I had a room in the college dorm and meals in the college cafeteria. I have always appreciated the benefits from the GI Bill, for me and for the others, many of whom were far more deserving than I. My relationship with Mom had, by now, evolved into trusted friends and confidants.

Since high school and early college years, I had not given much thought to a suitable career. While I was away in the Navy, I had dreamed mainly about coming home to the farm and my family. Now back in school, I had my hands full trying to get back into the swing of school work, especially in mathematics and science courses. I suppose that, had I been asked, I would have said one of my goals was, as before, to be a civil engineer, an uninformed choice, at best.

One day, toward the end of my junior year in school, I was asked to report to the dean's office. It has taken many years of retrospection for me to grasp or to acknowledge the full impact this call would have on the rest of my life.

With the dean sat a balding, portly man with an air of knowing what he wanted. The dean introduced him as Reverend Woods, the superintendent of Stafford, Oklahoma Schools. What the reverend wanted was for me to become the mathematics and science teacher and athletics coach of Stafford High school. Stafford, located about 10 miles southeast of my old hometown, was a very small village with a single grocery store. The salary was $1,300 per year for teaching with an added $100 per year for coaching. I asked if I might think about it for a day or so.

Why would this stranger offer me, a junior in college, such a job? I still held my high school teachers in absolute awe, especially someone like Mrs. Hackworth, my English teacher. I soon had a clue when I found out there were few qualified teachers after the war to fill teaching positions, especially in a small isolated community such as Stafford. Clearly, Reverend Woods was desperate.

When I went home that weekend, I asked Dad what he thought about the offer. He said in his knowing way, "Sonny that's an awful lot of money". All of which suggests the effects of the depression and the state of our family financial affairs over the preceding few years. I took the job.

I moved into a room at the rear end of the grocery store. Uncertainly, I bought my first car, a 1931 Model A Ford Coupe which I would drive home to Butler over the weekends. And the school year began.

Surprising for me, I fully enjoyed my year of teaching at Stafford. I found that I was as competent at teaching and coaching athletics as I was at farming or flying. I also discovered that teaching school filled my need to feel that I should do something positive and important with my life. This sense of purpose made easy work of teaching science without a laboratory and coaching in a gymnasium heated by two pot-bellied wood stoves, although I still have a burn scar on my left shoulder from an encounter with one of the stoves.

Some years later, I came to realize what my Dad's knowledge of financial futures had meant to me. I had selected a career that would be a guiding force for the rest of my life. He, ironically, had probably performed a service for me that few trained career counselors might have. It follows that I did not fare as well financially as he might have predicted.

Under my federal scholarship, I went back to college the following year to obtain my bachelors degree and appropriate teaching credentials. I spent several of my early years teaching and coaching in communities in western Oklahoma similar to Stafford, including a stint in my home town, with a continued sense of satisfaction and joy. The following account of my tour in the Putnam community is typical of these years of my life.

Living and Working in Putnam

The announcement posted in the teacher placement center at the college where I was attending Summer School stated that the Putnam, Oklahoma High school needed a mathematics teacher and athletic coach for the upcoming school year. I drove to Putnam to check on the opening, and in the rural vernacular, if I had blinked I would have missed it. Actually, I had grown up about 30 miles from Putnam but I had never purposefully been there, living on the other side of Barnitz Creek and toward Clinton, the hub city of western Oklahoma.

When I stopped at the one gas station in town to ask where I might find Mr. Joe Lawter, the school superintendent, one of the middle-aged brothers running the station said, "You mean Joe Blow?" He went on to tell me that the school was around the corner to the west. I hesitantly went to the school after this rather indirect, irreverent introduction to Mr. Lawter.

I located him in the school lunchroom, a wooden, one-room school building that had been moved in from one of the elementary school districts. I found a round, bald fellow with a cackling laugh working with another round fellow in overalls trying to mount a big exhaust canopy over the cook stove. Without introduction, they involved me in the final installation. They gave me the job of telling them when the lower edge was level with the stove. After several corrections, the guy in the overalls, apparently tired and exasperated, yelled, "Nail'er, Joe".

That was my formal introduction to the school superintendent and Sam Widener, the custodian. In time, the three of us were to become very close friends, and "Nail'er, Joe" became an important part of my private phraseology. Incidentally, Mr. Lawter was an excellent educator and a very supportive superintendent, and Sam the best counselor in the school.

They 'interviewed' me and hired me on the spot, not only as coach of all sports, but as the mathematics and science teacher - and as the school principal, as well. They then told me to go out to talk to the school board members, all farmers working in their fields, about my being the new coach. That gave me a hint as to who ran the school.

The board officially hired me at the next board meeting. The competition for the job apparently wasn't really keen, and affirmative action was far away on the horizon.

Teaching and coaching in a small town makes you extremely visible, both to the students and to the community. There is little privacy for you. A large percentage of students are engaged in athletics, and a large percentage of community members come to school events. They come, not because they have nothing else to do, but because they feel a kinship to the students and the school. I soon accommodated myself to the closeness of a school and community family.

Coaches in small schools have several things they must do, and the same, I am sure, applies to coaches in most urban schools. One must teach the players to act with courtesy, to play hard and try to win, and to win or lose with grace. You are not required to win; life is easier, however, if you do. Most community people know you, and it's much more fun to go to the post office after you have won.

There is a cliche that if a team one is coaching has little chance of winning, one builds character. People in Putnam had a good sense of our chances of winning particular games, and they were accepting of the teams' best effort. It was helpful to have a parent of one of the players remind you of the benefits of building character through your upcoming game with Leedey High school, a perennial state champion.

The major sport in most very small high schools is basketball. It's a fast-moving game, requires few players and is most often played inside during the winter months. The main objective in basketball is simply to gain an advantage over the other team, most often through a screen for a player to get a safe shot, a fast break, a confusing defensive tactic, or a clever throw-in play under your own basket, or players with stamina and a spirit to win. Of course, having tall players doesn't hurt your cause.

We worked hard to develop skills and strategies to win. Our teams held one practice session at night early in the season and invited everyone to attend. We demonstrated how we prepared to play our strategies to gain advantages and what spectators might watch for. It was fun to talk with grandmothers about "give and go".

I coached both boys and girls basketball in Putnam. I must say that I have seen few groups of young people who were brighter or more fun than these students. As a coach, there is little so uplifting as walking into a neighboring high school gymnasium with a team of youngsters you have taught and coached. Each has his or her own individual flair, walk, clothes, hair style, smiles... but they all have something in common; they have all been affected by you. In a way, they represent themselves, but they also represent who the coach is and what he or she stands for.

One year, the Custer City High School boys basketball team, during the regular season, had beaten our boys team unmercifully, by some 30 points. At the end of the season, we were to play them in the opening session of the district tournament. A group of our players took the time to scout Custer City playing another local team. They gave me a graphic report about how Custer City had won the game.

They theorized that Custer City's strength came from a large center's domination of the game under the basket, and the deadly shooting by a guard cutting across the free throw line. I was impressed that our players had such interest in their team and the insight to analyze a fairly complex set of activities. I also knew I had a special responsibility to help them solve a problem. We decided that we would play a four-man zone defense that would force Beberness, the hefty center, out from under the basket, while still covering the other players.

We assigned Speck Dodson the simple task of never letting Blankenship, the guard, move toward the free throw line. It embarrassed Speck for a while to stand to the side of an opposing player rather than between him and the basket. He forced Blankenship to go to the corner of the court rather than into his favored, deadly spot. During the game Blankenship scored but two points, and Beberness was a very frustrated young man.

It wasn't a difficult game for us to win, and there were many reasons to be proud of our team. They followed our defensive plan, took advantage of their own scoring opportunities, and played with spirit and stamina.

The Custer City coach, my good friend Tolbert Watson, was gracious and complimentary after the game. I, with some conscience, admitted that I had little to do with it all. I recall telling him it had to do with building character, which made absolutely no sense at that time to Tolbert following this particular game. The comment, however, was totally appropriate; we had won because of the character of our players, and, true to facetious form, we continued to build character through losing the very next game by a considerable margin.

TOM AND LOIS

When we were growing up, my oldest brother, Tom, and I seemed to have several trade offs, some I have associated with his being almost three years older than I. Tom worked in the hot fields with Dad, while I helped Mom in the cool farmhouse. At the time, wanting to be with Dad doing "man's work", I didn't appreciate my less masculine assignments.

In retrospect, Tom's rank as senior sibling resulted in his often coming up on the short end of the stick. As a teenager, Tom worked at Bowman's filling station, and on Saturday night while he worked, I usually drove the family car. My buddies and I often went off to the movie preview in Hammon in our car while Tom closed up the station. Tom was drafted into the Army and fought in the Battle of the Bulge during World War II. For service during the same war, I was embarrassed to receive a bonus for a cushy Naval flying assignment based at Guantanamo Bay, Cuba.

I have justified these trade offs by noting what a wonderful man he became. His rewards have been significant. He married Lois, the flower of the whole Butler area. We have a picture of her in her late teens holding a rose, and looking like the flower itself. She is still as lovely, given that our looks and tastes age wondrously together.

What a partnership! Tom and Lois have given unwavering support to one another and an equal sharing of the joys and tribulations of raising a wonderful family. I remember a time in Tecumseh, Oklahoma when they were both making sacrifices for Tom to go on to school. Lois was washing clothes and canning food of all kinds. Tom was selling products door to door. I asked him if their finances

were O.K., and he said they were in good shape, that they had 80 bucks in the sock. This kind of confidence has to come from a very firm base.

When Tom was in the Army, he loved to play cards, often with small wagers, I am sure. This seemed to almost everyone to be a justifiable diversion from the stresses of the times and its assignments. Back home, as Tom and I were talking about our lives, he said, perhaps tongue in cheek, had it not been for Lois he probably would have become a professional gambler. He no doubt came to this rather unlikely career possibility because of his success in taking considerable loose change from his fellow nephews of Uncle Sam.

I can hardly picture Tom now, with both of us in our declining years, wearing a green eyeshade and saying, "Burn one and deal".

FLAPPER

What weighed about 30 pounds, had blond hair, cost us nothing to acquire, yet was one of the best things to happen to our entire family? Her given name was Doris Ann Crowl, although we had a lot of endearing other names by which we addressed her. She lived with us five days a week while her mother went to college to learn to be a school teacher, and then for a while when her mom taught in a rural school to the north of us. Later on, we kept her with us whenever we could.

World War II was upon us, and our family was scattered because of the war. Doris Ann along with the younger members of our immediate family provided much of the comfort for my mom and dad during that period. Doris Ann was particularly close to Mom. One of my favorite photographs is of Mom standing on the front porch of our farm house, fly swatter in hand, and this pretty child sitting, smiling on a banister very close beside her.

Doris Ann became a member of our family. She had three natural siblings; Othal Dale, Jessie Ray and Judy, and she loved them dearly. But when she named her brothers and sisters, she included without pause; Tommy, Roger, Mary, Joe and J. T. She refers, yet, to Mom as Mama Duncan and to Dad as Daddy Duncan. She was our first introduction to a truly extended family. Weekends when she went back to her natural family lost some of their joy for us.

After World War II, we had a lot of changes in our family life. We sold our farm and moved into Butler proper, where Dad continued to buy and sell livestock. Part of the reasoning for the move was so that Dad would not tear up our rather rickety truck on daily trips on the rough dirt road out to our farm north of Butler.

We Duncan children settled into varied niches; Tom married Lois, I taught school and coached sports locally, and my younger siblings were growing up to do a variety of things. Doris Ann remained a constant. She sat on Mom's lap while Mom crocheted with her arms around her. Dad sang "Turkey in the Straw" while chording the piano with Doris Ann sitting beside him on the piano bench, and Doris Ann slept wherever there was space, with the sharpest pair of elbows and knees we ever knew. She was a best companion to bum around with, and we were all proud to be in her company.

Later my folks moved to Weatherford, Oklahoma as did I. Dad became the custodian of Stewart Hall, a girl's dormitory at Southwestern State College. Mom ran a boarding house for college students nearby. I married, and both my wife and I taught at the college.

Dad took great pride in his job, and he was particularly pleased when he could take Doris Ann with him as he did his chores. He gave her a great deal of latitude, letting her play in the dormitory attic with the accumulations of articles the girls had left behind. Doris Ann was his delight. He called her Flapper, a name he had given her at the very beginning of her staying with us on the farm.

Doris Ann remained a constant source or joy and pleasure for Mom. She was involved as only a child could be as Mom prepared and served food for college students who took their meals at Mom's table. The young men loved her, and the young women paid her a flattering amount of attention, involving her as they could in their lives.

I always enjoyed visiting with my folks and with Doris Ann when she was with them. She would often go with me when I taught classes at the college. Since my principal role was to prepare prospective teachers, I thought it most appropriate to take a child with me to the classroom. She recalls with some delight, her drawing on the chalkboard while I attempted to teach the classes. The Dean never objected, so I liked to assume that Doris Ann was helping fulfill some of the objectives of the college.

As years have gone by, our contacts with Doris Ann have become, quite naturally, less frequent as she entered school, grew up and became independent. She lives in Yukon, Oklahoma now, has her own family and feels close to her natural mother and her siblings. She is a competent and successful woman, personally and in the business world. I see her too infrequently, usually at functions involving my own family in Oklahoma or Kansas. But she has always been close to my heart.

She gives considerable credit to my family for her growth and survival in a rather uncertain and scary period of her life, but I can only imagine the impact on her. I know that her effect on us was profound. When I see her now, a beautiful caring woman, I see also the pretty child sitting, smiling close to the side of Mama Duncan on the porch of our old farmhouse.

MY FATHER'S LEGACY

Memories of my Dad are a special mixture of what he said and what he did. Some days he would be active, purposeful and energetic, and on others an unpredictable sluff-off and a very funny person. His effects on me were not always direct; he provided few models for me to follow. His influences were subtle, and perhaps for that the more persuasive.

Many of his influences on me to this day are the expressions he used to describe a situation or a condition. Perhaps it is like living by cliches, but a special set from a special source.   Dad was a fast walker. Even as a teenager, I often had to trot to keep up with him. If we were to walk some distance, to look at cattle he might buy or to take on a farm chore, and I complained about the distance or the speed, he would say, "Come on, Sonny, it's no distance for a stepper."

Dad was a "make doer", which could be interpreted as his being an unusual problem solver. He was indeed a pragmatist; if something worked, it was OK for all time. If a bull went through the wooden barnyard fence, he simply wired a spare wagon wheel in the hole in the fence. We had a strange looking barnyard fence, but it somehow fit in with the rest of the picture. Was it a contradiction when he would say to his children, "If it's worth doing at all, it's worth doing right"?

Dad never bothered much about appearances of the products of our work. His comment on the obvious flaws in one of our completed projects was usually, "It would never be noticed from the back of a galloping mule". Perhaps too often, I fall back on this wonderful release from the need to be perfect, as I apply the "Galloping mule criterion" to my efforts.

If we were working at a task such as digging a ditch in hard dry soil, often with inappropriate tools such as an axe instead of a pick, Dad would describe the soil as being "As hard as your mother-in-law's heart". The expression also was applied to a strong piece of old oak lumber we were trying to fashion into a double tree using the same dull axe. Incidentally, his mother-in-law was a dear, as he well knew. I have since found, on numerous occasions and in varied circumstances, the term to be a fun way to describe my feelings and my frustrations, with apologies to mothers-in-law everywhere.

During the winter months, we didn't have ready access to weather forecasts, or even an accurate, well placed thermometer. When we asked Dad how cold it was outside, he usually responded with his view of appropriate outerwear, such as, "About two shirts and a light jacket". Now when my daughter asks about the weather before she dresses for school, I modify his response with " I'd say, a long-sleeve shirt and a jacket".

Politically, Dad was a dedicated Democrat. His commitment to the democratic process at election time was to "Vote for the best man, provided he is a Democrat", which comments also on the male chauvinism in those times. When I asked him how he

voted, he would smile and say, "I just stamped the rooster," which I took that to mean he voted a straight Democratic ticket.

Not surprisingly, Dad as a farmer had mixed views about the right to live and to thrive. He had no compunction about our killing animals for family food, but he defended the rights of the wasps that had built a nest in the eaves of the roof of the house, saying, "All things have a right to live". This contradiction caused me to wonder if he was concerned mainly about our making the wasps angry by throwing rocks at their nest to dislodge it.

Dad had a real knack for turning aside some of our complaints with a wit all his own. One Saturday when I had been assigned the job of turning over the garden plot in the creek bottom with a walking plow, and he was taking brother Tom to the Elk City auction, I asked if I had to walk and plow all day, and he said, "Yes, unless you want to ride the handle bars."

I learned a lot of things from Dad, some very good and some not so good. I learned to work hard when life situations demand hard work. I will never forget the times I held a kerosene lantern for him to pick cotton after darkness had set in. I also learned to "make do", to slide by with temporary solutions to permanent problems.

Religion was not often a hot topic in our family, especially between Dad and the other members. We knew him to be a caring and ethical person, and we could predict how he would react to vital issues. In that sense, I suppose, he provided us moral and religious training, and in his own humorous way. A few weeks before Dad died, my oldest brother asked him, "Do you know where you will spend eternity?" Dad's philosophical response was a dry, "I reckon I'll soon find out".

Perhaps, the best part of my remembering Dad was his view that one should not take life too seriously, that the world doesn't have to be perfect, and a fun word can often turn a troublesome thing into a smile, though fleeting.

THEN AND NOW

In the 1930s, with shelter from the elements, with land to provide for most of our food needs, with kerosene fuel for lighting and heating, we felt ourselves to be as modern a farm family as our neighbors; we had everything we really needed for a comfortable life. As I look back on our life during that period, I marvel at our riches.

How swiftly times change. Fifty years later, I smile as I watch my family get up in the morning, turn up the thermostat and complain about the chill in the air as they delay taking a shower until the bathroom warms up.

In the 1930s there was no central heat in our house. There was a large stove in the living room, fired by wood, coal or anything else that was burnable. Later, in more affluent times, we used a kerosene stove, vented though the same chimney that had served the wood stove, and with a sort of automatic control of the amount of heat produced. Specific areas of the house were heated, rather than the entire house as it is today. Bedrooms were blocked off from the heat from the stove. When I went to bed in the wintertime, I slipped between soft flannel sheets and curled up in a ball to warm myself and the bed. A luxury was a hot water bottle or a warm brother.

On cold winter mornings, I would hear Dad get up and light a fire in the living room stove. I prayed that I had cut enough kindling and firewood for the stove, which was one of my family chores. In a bit, Dad would announce, "Fire's hot", and I knew it was time to grab my pants and shirt and head out to the stove, clad only in my scivvy shorts. We dressed around the stove, warming our clothes as we could before we put them on.

We surely would have been a strange sight for some, four boys trying to get their share of the heat with only our sister Mary and Mom dressed modestly. Our worst times were when Mary had a school friend sleeping over, and we had to emerge from the bedroom with at least our pants on. I somehow never thought about Dad's discomfort in putting on his cold clothes.

Our "bathroom" was an outdoor two hole privy, located on the far side of the chicken house. According to Mitch Jaynes of the Dillards folk singing group, in winter it was 50 yards too far from the house, and in the summer it was 50 yards too near. Sears catalogues often served as toilet paper, not always comfortable or efficient, but providing some interesting viewing and marketing. In other places and contexts, we referred to the catalog as the "wish book" where dreams were made and sometimes fulfilled. In the privy, one wished for softer tissue.

The privy wasn't really the bathroom; we bathed in either the kitchen or the living room, whichever was warmest. The bathtub was a No. 3 galvanized tub, hopefully the oval kind. As children, we took turns bathing, usually on Saturday morning before we went to town in the afternoon. Preference in the order of bathing was given to the younger family members, causing one to wonder at an early time in one's life about the problems of aging. In the summertime, a wash basin sat on a bench outside the kitchen door, with a bucket of water alongside accompanied by a bar of soap and a community towel hanging from the wall. In winter the operation was moved inside the kitchen. Brushing one's teeth involved taking a cup of water, a spot of baking soda on one's off hand, with a tooth brush out into the back yard for brushing, swishing and spitting.

We lit the house and read and wrote by kerosene lamps, usually at the kitchen table. Neither the intensity of the light nor the aroma at the table was commendable, but if you had a desire to learn, to communicate or to read for fun, they were acceptable. The lamps were filled each day, the wicks trimmed and the fragile glass chimneys carefully washed as we did the dishes.

We later bought a gas lamp, fueled with white gasoline. The light came from two mantles, about the size of large walnuts, that gave off a harsh blue light. It lit the house much better than before but somehow lacked the warmth of the yellow kerosene glow. Reading in bed was unheard of at our house because of the inconvenience of providing a lamp for each bedroom and the danger of fire (add the lingering odors of a cooling kerosene wick).

Mom made lye soap, heating fatty scraps of meat saved when we butchered hogs or trimmed pieces of meat, along with all the lard we had accumulated during the year. Because of the odors, we cooked this mess outside over a pile of wood. When it was all bubbly and the time was right, Mom would add the proper amount of lye, and stir it well. After a while, she would skim the residue from the top of the mess and spread the remaining concoction about 2 inches thick into available containers.

After the soap cooled, Mom would cut it into bar-sized chunks for storage and use. I have always wondered how Mom knew how much lye to put in. It would seem that adding too much lye could be real threat to the users of the soap. But the results from the use of Mom's lye soap were always positive, except for the odor. One year we stored the supply of lye soap under the bed Tom and I slept in. The soap had a distinctive presence, not particularly pleasant.

Clothes-washing day was a big event. Usually it was on Monday, which Mom began with an order that we would all change into clean clothes and pile the dirty ones in the middle of the kitchen floor. Dad often wryly complained to Mom that his undershirt was just beginning to fit. I don't recall our being a stinky family during the week; we simply from necessity were judicious about putting on clean shirts and dresses, knowing that doing laundry was a tough job, which usually fell to Mom, even with an energetic boost from the rest of the family.

Early in my life we did the laundry in two Number 2 galvanized tubs almost full of hot water. We set a wash board in one of the tubs, soaked the dirty clothes for a bit in the water and then scraped each article of clothing up and down on the washboard after rubbing P&G (Proctor and Gamble bar soap, also referred to as "Push and Grunt") or lye soap on the most soiled spots, pressing it down occasionally into the soapy water. The piece was then wrung out by twisting between one's hands. It was placed into the second tub of rinse water, sloshed about a few times, wrung once more and hung out on the clothesline to dry. The clothes smelled great when they were dry, like fresh air and sunshine.

In one of our later, more affluent years we bought a gasoline-powered washing machine. It sat in the kitchen, with its exhaust hose extended out the south window on Mondays. Its brand name was 'Dexter'; its putt-putt sound and the odor of the exhaust smoke are also lingering memories. We loved the crank operated wringer and that we could run the clothes through two rinses using our two No. 2 tubs.

It pleases me that wash boards now often serve as rhythm instruments in country music bands, a joyous association with

Monday wash days, and that clotheslines are referred to as solar clothes dryers.

There was something about those early farm days that continue to fascinate many of us. Today, we spend considerable amounts of money and a great deal of time to enjoy similar sets of deprivation by going to cabins in the mountains or camping out under primitive conditions. There is one added feature, however; we can always go back, at our whim, to the modern, comfortable lives we left momentarily. The difference between then and now seems to be a matter of convenience and choice.

EPILOGUE

There have been few persons or entities that seem to have aged more rapidly than I. The town of Butler has.

During the 30s and 40s, farms were relatively small, most within a range of 80 to 240 acres. That size farm was usually all that a family could effectively care for, unless a large portion of the land was kept as pastureland. Few, if any, farmers had motorized farm machinery. Almost all plowing and cultivating was powered by horse or mule pull and hand operated tools.

By necessity, the activities on these small farms were highly diversified to support the needs of their resident families. The needs of farm families helped create a market for a diversified center of trade to support them. Butler was well equipped to support its farm community.

But things changed... There was World War II and a rebounding worldwide economy to fill the gaps created by the war. There were technological advances that enabled farmers to become more efficient. The war forced or encouraged many people living on the farm or in town to go outside their community to a larger, different world, often never to return - or to plan a different kind of life for themselves.

One of the results of the war and its aftermath was that farms became larger. Consequently, the total farm population became smaller. As families left their farms, their land was bought by other farmers who had advanced mechanical equipment to care for expanded farm operations. A non agricultural bonanza came from large energy companies that competed for rather lucrative leases on farmlands in their search for oil and gas.

No longer was diversification a requirement for survival of a quality farm life. There was no longer a need to produce milk and eggs for an exchange market; you simply bought them in town from profits made from growing a large amount of cotton or grain in an efficient way. A new term was born... Agribusiness.

With the accessibility of comfortable, efficient cars and paved highways, it was easy to go to larger towns such as Clinton or Elk City to shop, where the offerings were more varied than in Butler and, through mass sales, less expensive.

There simply wasn't a need for a town such as the Butler of the 30s and 40s to support the farm community it had now become. Without the lifeblood that flowed from farms to town and back again to the farms, the life of Butler slowly faded and quieted.

In my later schooling, I learned that one of the major factors related to the decline of the mighty Roman Empire was the death or demise of the Latifundia, the farms granted to families in what is now basically Italy. Roman generals took farm men off to fight personal and national wars, and when the men returned from the wars, their farm lives were often no longer available to them. They settled in larger cities and became part of the populace that may have influenced politics, but did not contribute to the productivity of Roman life.

The parallels between the decline of the Roman Empire and the liveliness of Butler, Oklahoma may not be perfect. However, powerful external forces bring about inevitable changes in our lives. For example, with the competition of television, the attendance at an entertainment contest on a flatbed truck on main street on a Saturday night in 1993 would, I guess, be quite small. Crazy Elkins, who wrote the stirring, memorable song about the Washita Valley flood in 1934, would perhaps have a new content to write and sing about.

Many things about Butler remain the same. There is the same kindness and caring as before and which one does not have to earn. When my parents died, our family returned to Butler, all too briefly. Both Mom and Dad were buried in the Butler cemetery. There was an outpouring of kindness and support from the community, as one most often finds in a country setting.

As I look back, I am aware that my life too was swept along with the changes that came to Butler. I left Butler to pursue a life elsewhere, as did many of my childhood friends. Perhaps the need to meet our dreams, with the physical comfort set within them, exceeded the welcome of the intimate, honest encounters with nature that farm life in the 30s and 40s provided.

Oh, for the good old days!! As my brother would say, "A week of them would kill you". Except for the memories.

About the Author

Roger Duncan was born July 19, 1922 on a farm near Butler, Oklahoma. He grew up on the farm with his father, mother, three brothers and a sister. He graduated from Butler High School in 1940, and went on to earn his bachelor's degree at Southwestern State College in Weatherford, Oklahoma and his masters and doctorate in education at the University of Oklahoma in Norman.

Dr. Duncan was a navy pilot in World War II and a Coast Guard pilot during the Korean War. He taught mathematics and science in the Oklahoma public schools, where he also coached athletics. From there he went on to teach at Southwestern State College in Weatherford and Western State College in Gunnison, Colorado. He was Director of Development and Demonstration at the Colorado State Department of Education and retired in 1984.

Dr. Duncan lives and writes poetry and prose in Carbondale, Colorado where he also makes wooden toys, raises goats and chickens, keeps an eye on Mt. Sopris and tends his garden.

He is married to Brenda Duncan and has four children, Jennifer, Matthew, Nicola and Rachel and two grandchildren Emily and Duncan.

- Rick Frost